Fort Benning
Stories, Lies, and Legends

Bridgett Sharp Siter

To my favorite future son-in-law.
All the best!
Bridgett

SEVEN
INTERACTIVE

Dedication

This book is dedicated to Charlie Butler, or "Kid Butler" as he was called by the men he served alongside in the 504th Parachute Infantry Regiment. Charlie had barely started his senior year in high school when his number was called, and 18-year-old Charlie Butler, newspaper boy from Bessemer, Alabama, became Pvt. Charles Butler, Infantryman. The day a studio photographer came from Birmingham to photograph the Bessemer High Senior Class of 1944, Charlie was making his final training jump at the Fort Benning Parachute School.

Three months later, he jumped into Holland with the 82nd Airborne Division. He was the newest and youngest member of the 504th when C Company led an assault on the bridge at Nijmegan. Charlie told me he was too young and naive to be scared. He was injured that day and again at the Battle of the Bulge, but he survived to serve nearly 30 years, with multiple tours in Korea and Vietnam.

I met Charlie soon after I arrived at Fort Benning in 1999. He was 70 years old, an amateur photographer who volunteered his time and talent to the newspaper where I worked. We bonded over our shared love of history, motorcycles, photography and cranky humor. He finally let me interview him after I discovered *Those Devils in Baggie Pants*, a blow-by-blow account of the 504th involvement in WWII. We had the newsroom to ourselves, and Charlie let his guard down. He cried as he told me about war. "I try to block the bad stuff, but the twentieth of December is always a bad day," he said.

December 20 was the day C Company found itself on the outskirts of Cheneaux. As the newest member of the platoon, Pvt. Butler was expected to walk next to his squad leader as they approached the village, where they would meet head-on with German forces. At the last minute, he traded places with another soldier, a young man named Finkelstein. And you see where this is going.

Tears rolled down Charlie's face, but his voice was steady as he told me Finkelstein was killed when a 20-millimeter shell exploded his hand grenade and set him afire. "It talks about it in the book," Charlie said. "But it doesn't say he took my place." That was the only time I ever saw Charlie cry.

The last time I saw him back in 2005, I was the one crying, as I sat beside his bed and said goodbye. That night, cancer took Charlie from us. I still miss him.

Acknowledgments

First, thanks.

Thank you to my husband, Tom, who makes dinner so I can write.

Thank you, Sherry Dukes Roe, for inviting me to tag along on your adventures. That first one shaped my life.

Thank you to those who shared their stories and those who encouraged me to put these stories in a book. I am deeply indebted to those who helped me shape it and refine it, including my editors, Lori Vandergriff, Marty Johnson, and my daughter Brittney Beasley, whose gift for words far exceeds mine.

I tip my hat to my brilliant friends Jean Harron and Ed Howard, who taught me so much about Fort Benning history and tried to keep me straight when the line between legend and lie became fuzzy.

I am grateful to Rick and Caroline, my publishers, who made this process remarkably easy. Five stars! Would definitely recommend.

Thank you, Reader, for taking the time to hear me out.

And thank you, Jesus. Always!

Table Of Contents

Preface

By the time you read this, Fort Benning will be Fort Benning no more. Benning is one of several installations undergoing a name change in 2023. Still, these are stories of Fort Benning as this military installation was known in its first century. Let's meet back here in a hundred years to talk about the history of Fort Moore.

Introduction

My family came to Fort Benning in 1999, about halfway through my husband's Army career. We expected to stay two or three years and move on, as is the military norm, but here we stayed until he retired in 2008. We raised four children, and they're raising our grandchildren here. We both work on Fort Benning, and though we no longer live on the installation, if it is true as they say, home is where the heart is, Fort Benning will always be home.

More than 20 years ago, I was a reporter, and it was in that capacity I learned so much about Fort Benning history. I spent many hours in the newspaper archives and the basement of the Infantry Museum, and I interviewed an awful lot of people who knew Fort Benning history first-hand because they lived it. Most of them are gone now, and in some cases, they were my only source for specific information. That's why I use the word "legend" from time to time as I share stories that have been passed down through the years from one generation to the next.

I am not a historian, and this is not a history book. I'm a storyteller who enjoys history. This book is a collection of random stories, anecdotes and fun facts with a common setting. For want of a segue, I simply end one story and start the next and call it a new chapter. If that messes with your mind, you should buckle up. (If you're looking for a comprehensive book about Fort Benning history, I highly recommend *Home of the Infantry: The History of Fort Benning*, published in 2007 and written by Peggy Stelpflug and Richard Hyatt.)

History grounds us. It connects us to the land and the people who went before us and the community they created. That's my purpose as much as anything else, to make you feel at home, if only for a time. I hope you love it. (Fort Benning, I mean, not the book. The book is only marginally entertaining.)

CHAPTER ONE

God Willing and the Creek Don't Rise

Long before this land was Fort Benning, it was Kashita, the home of the Muskokee Tribe (later spelled Muscogee) of the Creek Indian Nation. The Creek Indians were the first we find living here in contemporary recorded history, but we don't know when they arrived. They descended from a nation that spanned what is now the Southeastern United States and became known as one of the Five Civilized Tribes. Kashita, meaning "peace town," was one of six major Creek towns within the confines of what is now Georgia and Alabama. The name of Cusseta, Georgia, a very short drive from Fort Benning, is a derivative of Kashita.

The Creeks left this area for several years to escape violent Spaniards and settled near what is now Macon, Georgia, and then returned and resettled on the land that is now Lawson Army Airfield to the west of Main Post. Most of what we know about the Creeks we've learned from the study of excavation sites at the airfield, which is naturally less disturbed by growth and development than Main Post.

The Creeks operated a floating bridge across the Chattahoochee River. In fact, they ferried Gen. Marquis Lafayette across the river at the end of his famous tour through Georgia in 1825.

The Federal Road passed right through what is now Main Post and served as the main traffic route for settlers moving from the Atlantic coast to the Lower Mississippi Valley. A historic marker on the western side of the airfield marks the spot where the Creeks ferried Lafayette across the river on his journey to Fort Mitchell, Alabama.

File this One Under Good to Know!

"God willing and the creek don't rise" is a bit of folk wisdom typically thought to mean someone is committed to doing something, assuming he or she is not hindered by any unforeseen circumstances or an act of God, as in, "I'll see you next week, God willing and the creek don't rise."

Contrary to conventional thinking, it is believed the phrase was originally literal, referring to the Creek Indians who populated this part of Georgia.

The first recorded use of the phrase is credited to Benjamin Hawkins, a politician and Indian agent (or diplomat) in the late eighteen and early nineteenth centuries. American Indians and the white settlers were constantly fighting for land, and diplomats like Hawkins had their hands full staving off conflicts and unruffling feathers, so to speak.

At some point, George Washington requested Hawkins' presence in the capital. In his response, Hawkins wrote that he would soon be on his way, "God willing and the Creek don't rise." His capitalization of "Creek" leads historians to conclude he was referring to the Muskogee tribe located in this area.

To protect the frontier, Fort Mitchell was built on the Federal Road in 1813. Shortly after the Battle of Hitchiti between the Creeks and the Georgia Militia in 1836 – the only battle ever fought on this land in recorded history – the Creeks of Kashita were carried across the river using their own ferry system and gathered at Fort Mitchell where they were forced to Oklahoma on the Trail of Tears.

After the Creeks were forced off their land, it was distributed by lottery, and Kashita became the Cusseta Plantation, sometimes referred to as Woolfolk's Hill, because it was owned by John Woolfolk, whose children eventually sold it off in parcels. It changed hands again and again until it was purchased by a wealthy Columbus businessman named Arthur Bussey, who built a summer home for his family in 1909 in the middle of his vast farm in the town of Shack, Georgia. That house he called Riverside, and it is now the centerpiece, the heart of Fort Benning. The town of Shack became the Main Post of Fort Benning.

One Way to Name a Place

SPEAKING of odd names for post offices reminds Leonard Lamb that Ft. Benning, Ga., used to be Shack, Ga., and that it came to be Shack this way: An office was to be established, and the government asked for suggestions. Many were sent in. Each time, however, a report came back that the names were too much like names of other post offices in the state. Finally Mr. Lamb says his father, sort of disgusted, wrote:

"Call it anything you like. The place is just an old shack, anyway."

Right back came the commission for Shack, Ga. And, the name stuck until the government established the army post there.

In 1938, the Knoxville Sentinel explained the naming of Shack, Georgia. The mercantile in Shack also served as a post office, and I've searched far and wide to no avail to find something with the Shack postmark. If you find something on eBay, I'll buy it from you at double whatever you pay, and we'll be BFFs.

Riverside, known as Quarters 1, was listed on the National Register of Historic Places in 1971. Though it was referred to as a plantation, it was never a plantation in the contemporary understanding of the word. Bussey built the house on a 1,782-acre plot he purchased for his farm. It was a bustling cotton, corn and sugar cane farm, with a dairy cooled by an innovative system Bussey designed to pump water up from a nearby spring. (The spring was later enlarged and dammed to form the pools that form Russ Park.) Riverside had a cotton gin, a trading post and housing for workers.

As for the house itself, the information provided to establish the home's provenance for the National Register said the "nucleus" of Riverside was a two-story meeting house built on Lumpkin Road in the early to mid-1800s. It was likely a multipurpose building used to host church services, school and civic events. The Columbus newspaper reported Bussey rolled the old meeting house on logs drawn by mules, and it was deemed an engineering feat that he didn't damage a single tree enroute to its new location on the farm that would become Riverside.

This view of Riverside shows the rear wing that was constructed around an "old meeting house" relocated to the property in 1909.

The meeting house was planted in place, and Bussey added forward and upward, including a parlor downstairs, bedrooms upstairs, bathrooms on both floors, and porches and verandas on three sides. Though Bussey called Riverside his summer home, he added three fireplaces, and the family spent at least two winters in the house. Today, that original meeting house serves as the kitchen at the back of the house, and though it is true that Riverside was built in 1909, the "nucleus" of the house is at least 50 years older.

If Native American history interests you, your bucket list should include a trip to Horseshoe Bend State Park in Daviston, Alabama, 76 miles from Fort Benning, and the Fort Mitchell National Historic Landmark, just minutes from Fort Benning in Alabama.

After Washington appointed Benjamin Hawkins as General Superintendent of Indian Affairs in 1796, Hawkins served as the principal agent to the Creek tribe in present-day Crawford County, Georgia. After 19 years of peace between settlers and the tribe, a group of Creeks known as Red Sticks rebelled against the European Americans. The civil war among the Creeks coincided with the War of 1812.

During the Creek War of 1813-1814, Hawkins organized "friendly" Creek Indians under the command of chief William McIntosh to aid Georgia and Tennessee militias in their fight against traditionalist Red Sticks. Gen. Andrew Jackson led the defeat of the Red Sticks at the Battle of Horseshoe Bend.

The Fort Mitchell National Historic Landmark is adjacent to the National Veterans Cemetery. The fort was built in 1813 by the Georgia militia in response to the violence between settlers and the two factions of Creeks I wrote about in Chapter 1. A visit here will fill in any gaps in that story. Here you'll see a segment of the Federal Road; what remains of those legendary "marker trees" that were said to serve as waypoints along native trade routes; and the starting point of the Trail of Tears.

CHAPTER TWO

A Cautionary Tale

A commemorative plaque stands behind Riverside on the corner of Kreis Street and Vibbert Avenue to mark the spot where once stood a creamery built by Arthur Bussey in 1915. When the Army purchased the property, the creamery was converted to serve as post headquarters until Building 35 was completed in 1935. Various services used the building thereafter.

The creamery had long housed the Office of the Staff Judge Advocate when it was burned to the ground in 2009. Sadly, in

The Infantry School Headquarters was housed for a time in the building that had previously served as the creamery for Arthur Bussey's farm. Historians believe the building was the third oldest structure on the post when it was destroyed in 2009.

addition to the loss of a historic building, nearly 100 years of military legal history was destroyed that night, including records of the controversial court martial trial that found Lt. William Calley guilty of premeditated murder at My Lai in Vietnam.

The arsonist was an employee facing disciplinary action for stealing office supplies. She set the historic building ablaze on a Friday night "in a fit of anger" at her co-workers.

Then she posted about it on social media. Then she went to prison for seven years.

CHAPTER THREE

Commonwealth

Before the land that is now Fort Benning was purchased by the federal government for the purpose of establishing a military post, these 182,000 acres were home to a number of communities, including a commune called Commonwealth.

The Christian Commonwealth Colony was an experiment in socialism based on the collective sharing of work and profits. On Nov. 1, 1896, colonists purchased nearly 1,000 acres 13 miles east of Columbus. Residents came from far and wide, but the majority came from Andrews, North Carolina, where a similar experiment had failed for lack of funding.

Members of Commonwealth disagreed on matters related to how the commune should operate, but they all agreed it should be

founded upon "unselfish socialism" and the practice of brotherhood. Work consisted mostly of farming, logging, and managing livestock and orchards. The residents tried and failed to generate income by operating a cotton mill, but they found some measure of success in the printing business.

From the start, the goodwill of the residents and the finances of the co-op were taxed by drifters and guests who lingered out of curiosity about the lifestyle. Members became less receptive to visitors and vagrants, and the Commonwealth open door policy was strictly modified in September 1898 to require visitors to work. No more freeloading in Commonwealth.

Commonwealth industry included logging, milling, and printing, but neither were sufficient to keep the community financially solvent.

In the summer of 1899, the experiment began to unravel when several members filed a lawsuit seeking compensation for their labor, claiming they were leaving the colony due to poor management and financial malpractice. They lost the case, but the incident didn't bode well for the future of the colony. After 44 months, Commonwealth fell into insolvency. Members stayed true to the founding principles of love and brotherhood, but they couldn't prevent economic collapse.

The population of Commonwealth peaked at nearly 500, but by 1901, the colony had disbanded, and the post office was transferred to the closest town, Upatoi. Ever notice you can rearrange the letters in Upatoi to spell Utopia? Turns out, those commune-ists were this close to paradise.

Learn more about Commonwealth in the *Georgia Historical Quarterly*, Vol. 57, published in the summer of 1973 by the Georgia Historical Society.

CHAPTER FOUR

Camp Benning

New military camps were being located all across the South in the early part of the last century. On April 4, 1917, the day after President Woodrow Wilson asked Congress for a declaration of war against Germany, the Columbus Chamber of Commerce began advocating for one of their own.

If Col. Henry Eames had his way, Fort Bragg would be Home of the Infantry. Eames led the board tasked to relocate the Infantry School of Arms from Fort Sill, Oklahoma, and he favored land near Fayetteville, North Carolina. Col. EP King, an artilleryman, beat him to the draw and claimed Fayetteville for field artillery training.

Columbus, Georgia, was Plan B. On August 27, 1918, the War Department decided to relocate the Infantry School to Columbus, and city officials were given two weeks to find adequate land and prepare it for the arrival of troops. About 84 acres "along the Macon Road" were deemed suitable, and an agent offered the owner one thousand dollars for a six-month lease. It's said the deal went down in a day, and the owner moved his family off the property by sunset, leaving behind a crop of sweet potatoes and cotton.

On October 5, Eames was named commandant of the new Infantry School of Arms. When the first troops arrived the next day, they found the land cleared and covered in tents, nearly 400 of them, used to house soldiers and serve as mess halls, offices and infirmaries. For nearly two years, the new installation was referred to as Tent City.

Anna Caroline Benning, the youngest daughter of the late Brig. Gen. Henry Benning, attended a ceremony to christen the new post "Camp Benning" on October 19. Naming the post after a Confederate slave-holding general seems like an odd choice today,

This 84-acre temporary troop encampment in Columbus was referred to as Tent City.

but the federal government had decided to name new military installations located in the south after Confederate generals as a conciliatory gesture aimed at assuaging any lingering bitterness in the decades following the Civil War.

It is said there were some in attendance the day Anna Caroline raised the flag over Camp Benning who remained staunch opponents of the federal government, and they heckled "Miss Anna" for her participation in opening day ceremonies. Her daddy would be so ashamed, they said.

It was soon obvious that the camp in Columbus was not big enough to accommodate the requirements of the Infantry post, so even as the temporary site was being constructed, federal officials were shopping for land. They found the land beside the river just south of Columbus ideal for their purposes, just as Arthur Bussey had found it ideal for his.

He didn't want to sell. In fact, he fought vehemently against it, until federal law enforcement officers showed up at his door to change his mind. Though he had asked for $878,000 and was still in the process of negotiating a deal, he was handed a check for half that amount and forced to vacate his property. When Bussey deposited a check in the First National Bank of Columbus for $439,000, it was the largest deposit in the history of the bank at that point.

Bussey and his tenants were forced off their land and given insufficient time to relocate property and holdings, resulting in the loss of livestock, crops, farm equipment and machinery. In 1930, Bussey filed for compensation in federal claims court. In Bussey vs United States, he asked the federal court to award him more than $108,700 and listed multiple grievances that painted Army officials as heartless and careless in their treatment of residents and livestock. I don't know the outcome of that case.

Then Peace Broke Out

Less than a month after Anna Caroline Benning ran the flag up the pole, the war came to an end. World War I, the war to end all wars. There was never going to be another war.

Maj. J. Paul Jones was the quartermaster responsible for camp construction. In January 1919, he received word that Congress had called a halt to construction on Camp Benning. When Jones read the order to "salvage Camp Benning," he ignored what he knew to be the intent of the order and settled on the dictionary definition of the word salvage: to save. Jones set about having buildings on the new camp painted immediately to "save" them, buying just enough time for proponents in Washington to convince Congress of the need for an Infantry School of Arms. By the end of January, Congress voted to resume construction, which had never really halted.

(Take a minute to appreciate the fact that a major was put in charge of building Fort Benning.)

Still, for nearly two years, Congress did what Congress does, which means they argued back and forth about whether Fort Benning should exist, whether they should fund permanent facilities and houses. Funds were frozen, funds were released. Then frozen again. Construction was a stop-and-go process.

Finally, on January 9, 1922, the War Department issued General Order No. 1 making Camp Benning a permanent military installation. Camp Benning was formally renamed Fort Benning.

Gen. John J. "Black Jack" Pershing was General of the Armies of the United States when he visited Camp Benning on December 10, 1919. With Pershing's visit came rains and floods so severe they sent local residents scurrying to their rooftops for survival. Rivers overflowed and thoroughly soaked the new camp, where most soldiers lived in tents and shacks. The event became known as the Great Pershing Flood. Two years later, in March 1922, Pershing returned for another visit, and once again, the rains came! The skies opened and dumped a deluge on the camp again in what was referred to as the Second Pershing Flood. It is said that Pershing commented that Camp Benning seemed an ideal place to train the Navy.

CHAPTER FIVE

Mr. Betjeman Goes to Washington

When news reached Columbus that the Infantry School of Arms would leave Fort Sill, city officials enlisted John Betjeman to go to Washington to promote Columbus as the ideal location for a military installation.

Betjeman was said to be a born ambassador, an outgoing young man who won the hearts of the Columbus community soon after he moved here in 1917 to manage the Jordan Company. ('J-ur-dun' rhymes with burden, not like Michael or his shoes. It takes some getting used to.)

With Fayetteville out of the running, Columbus became the first choice for the Infantry School, and Betjeman worked tirelessly to make it happen. On August 27, 1918, the War Department gave him the nod, and Betjeman returned to Columbus to share the good news. He was feted at a banquet and presented a silver loving cup and a check for $2,500, which would be nearly $50,000 today.

On Sept. 22, 1923, Fort Benning celebrated the dedication of the Upatoi Bridge with a formal procession across the river that included the post commander, the mayor of Columbus, five tanks and a Howitzer. For many years, the bridge served as the primary access and egress from Fort Benning, with a two-lane road, a foot path and railroad tracks leading from Fort Benning to Columbus. The road was not paved for two more years.

Betjeman died at the age of 44 in 1924 and was buried in Linwood Cemetery in Columbus. In 1937, a new concrete bridge replaced the original wooden bridge that served as the main access

Fort Benning celebrated the dedication of a steel trestle bridge across the Upatoi River in 1923. The bridge replaced a crude wooden structure built before the land was purchased for military use.

and egress between Fort Benning and Columbus, and the new structure was dedicated to him.

While the Army was busy building the fort, Columbus went to work on Benning Boulevard, which would serve as the main road to Fort Benning for many years. The boulevard replaced a "washboard" dirt road that had previously made travel between the city and the camp a tedious and lengthy process. The completion of the road in 1925 "sealed the union" between the two communities.

City officials decided to celebrate the union, and a handshake wouldn't suffice. It was to be a wedding ceremony. On June 2, 1925, officials from Columbus met leaders from Fort Benning at the Springer Opera House in Columbus. Judge C. Frank McLaughlin represented the bride and Col. A.B. Warfield stood in as the groom in the absence of Brig. Gen. Briant Wells, who was traveling at the time. The 29th Infantry Band played the Wedding March, and Congressman W.C. Wright officiated.

The newspaper reported "a real honest-to-goodness kiss" sealed the vows, and Wright ended the nontraditional ceremony with a traditional exhortation: "What the paved road has joined together, let no man put asunder."

Betjeman Bridge is pictured here with in-bound and outbound lanes, railroad tracks and a sidewalk.

CHAPTER SIX

Evolution of the Camp

Though military installations are often collectively referred to as bases, the Army traditionally uses the word "post." If you mention to someone locally that you live on base, he will assume you are new to the Army or you are an Air Force family assigned to Fort Benning. A hundred years ago, you would have used the word "reservation," but time and cultural sensitivities have skewed the definition of the word.

Whatever you call it, a military installation by any other name is still a camp. In the early years, one might have referred to it as a troop encampment, which is a broad definition for any place soldiers might bed down for the night. Today we use the word "cantonment" to describe a military garrison.

Building 35 was built in 1935 to serve as headquarters for the Infantry School.

The evolution of the name Fort Benning looks something like this ...

• *Camp Benning was established in Columbus in October 1918 and relocated to its current site soon after, out of need to expand the Infantry School of Arms. It was named for Confederate Brig. Gen. Henry Lewis "Old Rock" Benning.*

• *On January 30, 1920, the new school was unarmed, when the Infantry School "of Arms" became the Infantry School.*

• *In 1922, Camp Benning became Fort Benning, when Congress authorized the camp be made a permanent installation.*

• *The Home of the Infantry became the Maneuver Center of Excellence in 2011, after the Base Realignment and Closure Commission decided to relocate the Armor School from Fort Knox, Kentucky. The Commission first intended to move the Infantry School to Fort Knox, because moving boots is much easier than moving tracked vehicles, but as it turned out, the topography there wasn't conducive to expansion and Infantry training. Once again, Fort Benning was Plan B.*

• *If all goes as planned, Fort Benning will become Fort Moore in the next couple of years to honor the late Lt. Gen. Hal Moore and his wife Julia. You'll read about the Moores later on.*

Later land acquisitions expanded the installation to include 182,000 acres and three more cantonments: Kelley Hill, Sand Hill and Harmony Church. Think of them as cities within a city.

Building 35 was built to serve as the Infantry School headquarters in 1935 during the Depression-era period of massive government spending. The original Infantry School was lauded as the largest federal office in the southeast upon completion, with floor space equal to that of a 10-story building. It was painted olive drab at first ("OD green" is Army green, the most common natural color for concealment and camouflage in foliaged environments), but the supervising architect ordered it repainted immediately, and today old timers* refer to it as the Big Pink Building**. It was the Infantry School and post headquarters until 1964.

Various organizations took up residency in Building 35 throughout the years. Today, it houses a variety of services and agencies, including most services for in- and out-processing. It is considered a public building, so a visit to this gorgeous facility should be on your Fort Benning Bucket List.

Building 4, the new Infantry School headquarters, was dedicated on June 5, 1964. In preparation for the event, the Infantry flagstaff was removed from Building 35 and installed in front of the new six-story, $10 million facility, which took two years to complete. With access to closed-circuit television, it was the first military school to use telecasts as a teaching aide.

These images show the post flagpole being lowered at Building 35 and raised in front of the new headquarters building in 1964.

Infantry Hall was designed in a stark mid-century style with very narrow windows. It was covered in pale yellow bricks and looked very different than it does today.

Building 4 is now McGinnis-Wickam Hall. More than $172 million was invested in major renovations, resulting in a facade that better matches the historic Main Post aesthetic, various sustainable features, and a more economic use of interior spaces.

* Me. Just me.

** It's not pink, but it has pale blush undertones that give great pink vibes.

Infantry Hall, the New Infantry School Headquarters, was dedicated in 1964.

Eighty percent of the materials removed from the original building were recycled, helping this facility earn a LEED Gold certification (Leadership in Energy and Environmental Design.) It is six stories high, covers 12 acres and contains more than a half a million square feet of floor space.

The façade of Infantry Hall was redesigned to compliment the historic post esthetic when the building was renovated and redesignated McGinnis-Wickam Hall.

Who says history doesn't repeat itself? In June 1932, the tank school moved from Fort Meade, Maryland, to Fort Benning, and Infantry School students were given basic tank instruction. Tank students often combined instruction with community chores, like driving the tanks to collect garbage around post. The *Army, Navy Register* reported, "The location of the two schools at Fort Benning is regarded as one of the most important steps made in recent years toward improving the facilities for training the infantry." The Harmony Church area of post was casually referred to as Camp Tank until tank training ended at Fort Benning in 1940, when the Armor School opened at Fort Knox.

CHAPTER SEVEN

He Made Better Dogs of Us All

"Branches of an ancient oak sweep over a gentle rolling hillside plot near the banks of the Chattahoochee at Fort Benning, marking ground set aside for the burial of pet dogs."

So began an article penned by Ed Sullivan in the Chattahoochee Canines column of the *Columbus Ledger* in 1958, just over a year after the Women's Club of Fort Benning broke ground in March of 1957 on a half-acre of land on 10th Division Road on the northern border of Main Post.

Today the spot bears a sign that reads "Animal Cemetery." And today it is full, but at the time of Sullivan's writing, only 97 dogs had been buried there. It was believed the spot would eventually accommodate the remains of 750 dogs, but by the time burials "officially" ended in the mid 1990s, the cemetery contained nearly a thousand family pets, 49 scout dogs, a handful of cats, and a sheep.

Among the first to be buried there was Butchie, the beloved pet of Maj. Gen. H.B. Powell, the post commander, who had only recently given permission to the Women's Club to create a pet cemetery, which was a rarity on U.S. military posts back then.

The remains of one of the most famous scout dogs followed soon after. Twelve-year-old York, a Korean War hero who was said to have nine years of active duty and nearly 150 combat patrols to his credit, was nearly deaf and mostly blind when he was struck by a truck Aug. 13, 1957. He was buried on the south side of the cemetery in the shade of that giant Red Oak to which Sullivan referred in his Chattahoochee Canines column. Two plaques were laid flat in the earth to mark the spot with distinction worthy of the war hero who had earned the Distinguished Service Award.

About that sheep. Old Faithful was a blood donor for Martin Army Hospital's laboratory, where his blood was used in diagnostic testing from 1945 to 1959. When Old Faithful died at the age of 14, he was buried with honors, including various posthumous awards and citations.

At one time, someone somewhere kept a list of burials there, probably someone at the post veterinarian's office, since they took charge of burials and marked the graves. Many of those markers have been lost to time and weather and mower blades, but a few notables remain, including:

• General Rebel Lee, Aug 2, 1951 - Feb 10, 1967, A true soldier and loved best friend. You will remain forever in our hearts.

• Beloved Nishka, Westie, 16 Apr 76 - 22 Sept 81, He didn't drown, he died swimming.

• Niki USAIC MP CO Sep 83 - Jun 88 Killed in the line of duty

• Bell-Bell, The Sociable Cat

• Twinkles, My Best Friend

There have been a few rogue burials over the past few years, including poor Buddy, who was inadvertently (I hope) buried on top of another grave in April 2016. Please be aware that the cemetery is full, and most graves are simply unmarked, or markers have been displaced over time. Please don't do that to your Buddy.

Calculator

You know who isn't buried in the Fort Benning Animal Cemetery? Calculator. No one knows where Fort Benning's most famous dog is buried.

Though it was said "his bloodline was questionable, Calculator was a true-blue patriot" and a constant companion of Fort Benning soldiers on post and off. No one knew where he came from, and no one could claim ownership. Calculator slept all around the post, and on weekends he would hitch a ride to Columbus. Sunday evening, soldiers driving back to Fort Benning would pause at the Ralston Hotel in Columbus to see if Calc needed a ride back to post. He was loved by all and considered to be the post mascot.

This is the only photo of Calculator known to exist. A painting of the dog hangs in the National Infantry Museum (and the museum should be on your Fort Benning Bucket list!)

Calculator was named for his distinct walk. It was said he "walked on three and carried one." Because he often "changed legs" midstride, some believed the mutt was calculating in the sense that he set out to elicit sympathy. Others said he was named for the mathematical practice of adding double digits in a stacked column form. (For instance, when adding nine plus four, you "drop three and carry one.")

On August 29, 1923, Calculator died after consuming strychnine, commonly called rat poison and commonly used in the early days of Fort Benning to keep vermin at bay. One would assume it was an accidental death, but the Fort Benning community was livid and considered the tragedy murder.

Shortly after his death, the post newspaper ran an article asking soldiers who knew and loved Calculator to donate a quarter to fund a memorial. More than 1,000 quarters, 16 pesos and eight gold pieces came in from around the country.

Calculator's memorial was originally located on what is now Stilwell Field on Main Post. It has been moved several times.

The article said, "Let this monument stand as a permanent testimonial to the admonition that unkindness to dogs will not be tolerated by the Infantry. Our late President Harding took an oath never to kick a dog; and this monument will stand as a pointing finger of warning to those inhuman morons who throw all the dictates of love and affection to the winds and kill one of the best friends man has, the dog — a real pal. Let this monument stand, too, as a testimonial to the love and affection with which the Infantry School regarded dear-old Calc – let it be symbolic of a permanent half-mast in honor of a dead companion."

After an unexplained delay, the memorial was finally erected in 1930 in the middle of the academic area near the post flagpole, where Stilwell Field is today. The post newspaper, in a report about the monument dedication, said "The mystery of his murder was never solved."

The granite memorial is inscribed with the words, "Calculator – Born? Died Aug. 29,1923/He Made Better Dogs of Us All."

In 1935, the monument was moved to the new Infantry School, Building 35. Around 1990, it was moved to the Infantry Museum, when the museum was located on post. In 2012, it was moved to Sacrifice Field, and finally, in 2015, back to Building 35. Still, no one knows where Calculator was buried.

Furlough

There is another monument on Fort Benning dedicated to a dog, a Dachshund named Furlough who served as the mascot of the 551st Parachute Infantry Battalion from December 1942 to December 1944, when he went missing in Belgium. The figure of a Dachshund stands at the foot of the 551st memorial on Sacrifice Field.

Enroute from Fort Benning to Panama in December 1942, the Solders of the 551st stole the puppy from the fenced yard of the port commander at Camp Patrick Henry in Virginia. They reported Furlough narrowly escaped death in 1943, when he was discovered aboard the ship headed back to the states and ordered overboard by the ship's master-at-arms. The battalion commander went toe-to-toe with the master-at-arms to save the dog.

They also said Furlough was lost in transit as the unit maneuvered through Belgium during the Battle of the Bulge. He was listed as missing in action.

I don't believe it. I choose to believe the soldiers who loved Furlough so much they would fight for his survival, and later erect a monument in his memory, were careful to find him a safe haven – perhaps another fenced yard in a village in Germany – before they went into battle. Furlough probably has great grandpuppies running all over Germany.

That's my story, and you can't change my mind.

Furlough's memorial is located at the foot of the 551st monument on Sacrifice Field.

CHAPTER EIGHT:

Miki

It boggles the mind, the things soldiers got away with not so long ago. The 515th Parachute Infantry Regiment kept a lion as a mascot in 1943 until she became too hard to handle. The commander of the 517th Parachute Infantry Regiment at Toccoa, Georgia, sent Miki, the young lioness, to the commander of the 515th as a practical joke.

At first, Miki was said to be "gentle as a kitten and likes to romp with the paratroopers who now are getting over their first awe of the 300-pound animal." The soldiers of the 515th built a cage for the big cat and vowed to take her to war with them.

It soon became obvious that Miki couldn't stay when she took a playful swat at a young soldier and sent him to the infirmary for stitches. I can find no record of what became of her, but I suspect she found a new home at a zoo somewhere in the Southeast.

Miki the lioness was perhaps the most unusual mascot in the history of Fort Benning.

CHAPTER NINE

Deer Billy

Dogs and cats get all the good press, but a buck made headlines in 1934, when three deer were shipped to Fort Benning by First Lt. L.S. Graham, a student at the Infantry School, who had raised the buck named Billy and two does at Fort Sam Houston in Texas. That's probably not legal now.

The deer arrived by train and were turned loose on the installation several weeks before Graham arrived with his family, which included a 9-year-old son named Bruce. Despite their best efforts, Graham and his son could not find the does, but Billy the buck came bounding out of the woods when Bruce whistled and offered a lump of sugar.

The newspaper reported that Billy trotted alongside when Bruce rode his bicycle around post. He ate from the boy's hand and slept cuddled up with the family's dog.

Please Don't Fry the Fish

In 1938, hunting and fishing regulations on Fort Benning included the following:

• No fishing with grenades or other explosives.

• No fishing with firearms.

• No fishing with poison or India berries.

• If you planned to hunt with hounds, you were required to first notify the Provost Marshal.

• No hunting on Sundays.

• No hunting with firearms "oftener than three days a week."

• Bobcats and foxes were not to be molested in specified areas.

• There was a $.25 bounty on the head of each wild domestic cat, considered vermin, and "any loose house cat will be construed as a wild domestic cat if found more than 100 yards from an occupied dwelling." Fair game.

CHAPTER 10

Airborne All The Way

How did they come to be there, those iconic training towers on Main Post?

In 1935, Amelia Earhart was the first person to make a public jump from an airborne training tower in the United States.

The Soviets were way ahead of us, having recognized the need for military parachute forces early in the twentieth century. In the crude wooden structures the Russians were using in the 1920s, Earhart saw potential for emergency bailout parachute training for

Parachute Jump Training Towers are pictured here on the cover of a pamphlet published in the 1940s.

Photo Courtesy of Switlik Survival Products

aviators. She and her husband, promoter George Putnam, partnered with Stanley Switlik, owner of the company that designed the parachutes Earhart used during her famed flights, to erect a 110-foot jump tower on Switlik's farm in New Jersey (which would later be the site of Six Flags Over New Jersey).

In order to generate public interest in the potential for airborne training, they invited the media to attend the maiden jump on June 2, 1935. Earhart, a media darling and an American hero, described the descent as "loads of fun."

The Coney Island Parachute Jump, which became known as the Eiffel Tower of Brooklyn, was relocated to Coney Island in 1941. There it remains, though no longer in use, having been designated as a landmark and listed in the National Register of Historic Places. It is occasionally lit up to commemorate an event, such as the tragic death of Kobe Bryant in 2020.

After Earhart went missing in 1937, Putnam lost interest in the endeavor, so Switlik took on another partner, retired Naval Commander James H. Strong, who had already experienced success

The 250' tall Coney Island Parachute Jump was designed by James H. Hall, whose Safe Parachute Company erected four training towers at Fort Benning.

with a 250' jump tower he designed for the World's Fair in New York. Unlike the airborne training tower that was designed to acquaint the user with the experience of freefalling under a canopy, Strong's tower was a "controlled descent" experience designed for entertainment only.

Strong's design for a tower included eight guide wires circling a parachute. He founded the Safe Parachute Company and constructed several demonstrations towers.

PARACHUTE   TEST   PLATOON

1ST ROW, L-R — HALEY   KELLY   SMITH   WARD   KITCHENS   IVY   POUDERT   PETERS   McLANEY   COLEY   MONTISETT   SHEPHERD

2ND ROW, L-R — CORBIN   BURKHALTER   ROBERTS   BROWN   KING   RUTLAND   HARDIN   McCULLOUGH   KASELL   DODD   WILLSON

3RD ROW, L-R — VOILS   GUILBEAU   PITTS   DOUCET   LT. RIDER   LT. BASSETT   W/O WILSON   WALLACE   HARRIS   WADE   PURSLEY   DAVIS   SKIPPER

4TH ROW, L-R — REESE   ROBINSON   JACQUAY   CORNELLIOUS   SELMAN   KIRKSEY   EBERHARDT   WEEKS   BOROM   ADAMS   TRACY

ABSENT — BROWN, L.   ORLBURN   ELLIS   HOUSTON   KETCHERSIDE   SWILLEY   WILLSON, O.   YATES

In 1940, with war raging in Europe, the U.S. Army decided it was time to train soldiers in airborne operations, and 48 enlisted men were selected from the 29th Infantry Regiment at Fort Benning to form the original Parachute Test Platoon. Requirements were stiff. Volunteers were required to have served at least two years in the Infantry, weigh no more than 185 pounds, be in excellent physical condition and be unmarried, due to the inherent danger.

And here I pause to editorialize. In my experience as a reporter, having interviewed many, many soldiers from every war since WWII, no one ever struck me as any braver than the young men who volunteered to jump from an airplane when it had never been done in this country. Not a single one of them had ever even flown on an airplane.

The entire test platoon was shipped to New Jersey to train on those jump towers erected for demonstration, and when they returned unscathed, the Army purchased four towers of their own. The Safe Parachute Company installed the first two towers on Eubanks Field in 1941 and two more in 1942. One was toppled in 1954 by a tornado that devastated the Chattahoochee Valley (and killed a child and a soldier on Fort Benning).

The towers are arguably the most widely recognizable symbol of Fort Benning, even more so than the Follow Me Statue and even among the civilian population that has never set foot on Fort Benning, partly because they have served as the backdrop for several movies. Read more about those movies in Chapter 21.

This miniature chapel was built in 1922 by a Fort Benning soldier known only as Pvt. Stadnik of the 29th Infantry Regiment, who constructed the shrine behind the Fort Benning stables out of gratitude for his recovery from a serious illness. The small cathedral, with three carved towers no more than six feet tall, was just large enough inside for one man to kneel at a hewn altar. The chapel was dedicated to Saint Hubert, patron saint of horsemen, and to former members of Fort Benning's military riding classes who died in battle. Vandals eventually destroyed the tiny chapel.

CHAPTER 11

Geronimooooo!

In August 1940, a brave group of young American soldiers volunteered to jump from a perfectly good airplane for the very first time. You met the Original Test Platoon in Chapter 10.

On the night before the first jump onto Fort Benning's Lawson Airfield, several of them watched a movie at the Main Post Theater to distract themselves from their nervousness. It was a western movie about the cavalry's search for the Apache chief Geronimo.

Afterward, Pvt. Aubrey Eberhardt vowed to prove he wasn't "scared out of his wits by yelling 'Geronimo' as loud as hell when I go out that door tomorrow."

Eberhardt was true to his word and followed with what he called "an Indian war whoop." In doing so, he unwittingly originated what would become the unofficial cry of the American paratrooper, Geronimo!

In July 1934, Fort Benning celebrated the grand opening of the new Fort Benning Officers' Club, which featured a beauty parlor, grill, reading room, barber shop, lodging upstairs and a lounge for men that was off limits to women. It also featured an innovative loudspeaker system, something new around these parts. When they put the loudspeaker to use during the grand opening celebration, it sent ladies scurrying from the powder room in a panic. A post official reminded guests the club would only stay grand so long as members didn't carelessly leave their "smoldering butts on the windowsills."

CHAPTER 12

A Thing Possessed

In 1943, an instructor from Fort Benning's Parachute School "made a leap into Alabama" near Fort Mitchell and landed in a farmer's field on top of Nancy, a hollow-horned goat.

The canopy shrouded Nancy, who flew into a rage, shredding the parachute and "dancing around like a thing possessed," the instructor told a reporter. By the time he freed her, the goat and the paratrooper had made peace.

Soon after, the farmer presented Nancy as a gift to the Parachute School, where she roamed freely on the grounds, decked out in a red jacket sewn by the school's parachute riggers.

CHAPTER 13:

Triple Nickels

We were a segregated Army. When First Lt Benjamin O. Davis Jr. lived on Fort Benning from 1936 to 1938, the future commander of the Tuskegee Airmen was the only black officer living on post. With no housing available for black officers, post officials tucked him and his wife into the corner unit of the last red-brick duplex on McIver Street, but he was not allowed to socialize with his neighbors at the Officers Club or the Main Post Theater.

Today, 301 McIver Street is marked with a bronze plaque and dedicated to the memory of a man who served his country proudly and overcame incredible obstacles to earn the rank of four-star general.

The McIver complex was built in 1923 and named for the late Brig. Gen. George Willcox McIver, who served as the commandant of the School of Musketry in Monterey, California, from 1907 until 1912. The School of Musketry was a predecessor to the School of Infantry. McIver was considered more progressive than his peers, and he worked to integrate military units with Native American and African American soldiers. He died in 1947 and is buried in Arlington Cemetery, but he lived long enough to see McIver Street named for him.

Across Main Post, those darling white cottages on Indianhead Road were assigned to the black NCOs of the 24th Infantry Regiment in the 1930s and 1940s. First Sgt. Walter Morris lived there at 302 Meehan Street from 1943-1944.

Morris was in charge of the soldiers who maintained the Airborne training area after duty hours. Morale was low, Morris said, so he started drilling them in the evening hours, putting them through a facsimile of the Parachute School's conditioning course. One night, the commandant, Lt. Gen. Ridgely Gaither, drove by and saw "50 black soldiers jumping up and down shouting, 'one thousand one, one thousand two'."

When Gaither called him to his office the next day, Morris feared he was about to be fired.

Instead, Gaither confided in him that a new, all-black parachute company was being formed, and the general invited Morris to be the first sergeant in the outfit.

"I was elated," Morris said. "My heart almost burst."

The 555th Parachute Infantry Company was activated soon after, and on February 16, 1944, the first class of all black, volunteer paratroopers graduated at Fort Benning.

Today, 302 Meehan Street is listed on the Black History Trail and distinguished with a bronze marker that identifies Morris as the first black soldier selected for parachute duty and the first Senior NCO of the 555th Parachute Infantry Company – the Triple Nickels.

First Sgt. Walter Morris is pictured with his family in front of their house on Fort Benning.

In 1948, President Harry S. Truman signed an executive order desegregating the military.

This picture was taken at Doughboy Stadium in 1929 during one of several visits Franklin Delano Roosevelt paid to Fort Benning when he was the governor of New York. Warm Springs, Georgia, was FDR's home away from home. The warm spring waters of Pine Mountain offered relief from the lingering effects of the polio he had contracted as an adult. His "Little White House" is now open to visitors, and it should be included on your Fort Benning Bucket List.

CHAPTER 14

Cemeteries

Fort Benning officials and an incredible group of volunteers have numbered and catalogued more than 60 cemeteries on the post, and all of them, except the Main Post Cemetery, existed before the land was acquired by the Army. They belonged to the families, churches and communities that went before.

The cemeteries are mowed from time to time, but mostly they're left in peace. Post officials are responsible for basic maintenance, but little can be done about the damage wrought by time. If a family wishes to visit the grave of an ancestor that is located near a range or in a hunting area, post officials will work with them to schedule a time when it is safe to do so and in some cases even escort them to the site.

In this chapter, I'll tell you more about three cemeteries that are easily accessed and "open" to the public in so much as visitors are not restricted. All three are fenced. Park alongside the road at cemeteries 2 and 7, wear good walking shoes and watch your step. Please be mindful that not all graves are marked with headstones, and several headstones have been displaced. Occasionally, visitors leave tokens or trinkets on graves; please leave them be.

Cemetery #7

The cemetery in the Harmony Church cantonment area is the McBride Cemetery, Cemetery #7, located just off 1st Division Road, and it is all that remains of the community that grew up around the Harmony Methodist Church, which was built on the site in the 1800s when land was deeded to church trustees, including James McBride. The McBrides were prominent Chattahoochee County pioneers.

It is quite likely that James McBride is buried in this cemetery, though there is no marker to indicate that is true. His son, William J. McBride, was buried here in 1898. He served in Pemberton's Company of the Georgia Cavalry of the Confederate States of America. His son, also William J. McBride, also served in Pemberton's Company, and the two have identical headstones rising high above those that surround them. The younger McBride was buried here in 1916. Alongside him is his wife and six of their eight children. Two of his kids, Clinton and Elvie, died of typhoid three weeks apart in 1916, the same year their father died.

That left William's sister, Annie Florence McBride, all by herself. She never married and presumably had no form of income and no future when she took her own life in 1927 at the age of 51 while living in a rooming house in Columbus. Her death certificate said Annie died by "suicidal intake" of gas.

Cemetery #2

Cemetery #2 is closer to Main Post and hidden in plain sight on a hill alongside Santa Fe Road, sandwiched between Love Dental Clinic and the PX in what was once a tiny farming community known as Redbone. I'm told the community was likely named for the Redbone Coonhound, a breed of hunting dog, but the word was also historically slang for a Native American or a person of mixed race.

The Parkmans were Chattahoochee County pioneers, and by the time the federal government absorbed their land, the Parkman family farmhouse had stood for 100 years on the hill where now stands the shell of the former Martin Army Hospital.

David Richard Parkman and his wife, Anna Cordelia, were loath to part with their land, but the government gave them no choice. They were allowed to live on the homestead until David's death in 1921, but they were not buried in the family cemetery. Some say they were not permitted to be buried on post, because it was federal land, but I cannot find proof of that. There were burials on post in private cemeteries long after the land was acquired by the Army. It's possible the policy prohibited civilian burials early on and then changed. Whatever the reason, David and Anna Cordelia are both buried in Columbus in Linwood Cemetery.

There are about 20 distinguishable graves in Cemetery #2. Perhaps there are more, but age and weather have left their exact location a mystery. A heap of what appears to be headstones surrounds a mound of dirt, leaving one to assume they once marked rows of graves.

Across the graveyard, time has eroded the red clay into a steep but shallow bank, much too close to the grave of William H. Parkman, who served, according to his epitaph, in Pemberton's Company of the Georgia Cavalry of the Confederacy, just as the McBrides had done. Pemberton was Lt. Col. John Stith Pemberton.

Who was Lt. Col. Pemberton?

The last land battle of the Civil War, the Battle of Columbus, was fought along the Chattahoochee River between Columbus, Georgia, and Gerard, Al., (which is now Phenix City) before the sun came up on Easter Sunday in 1865. Today it is known as the Battle of Columbus, but historians often refer to it as Wilson's Raid. Gen. James Wilson led Union forces in a march across Alabama and into Georgia in an attempt to bring the Confederacy to its knees by destroying supply centers in Selma, Alabama, and Columbus, which was home to an arsenal, an iron works factory and a naval yard.

Union troops took Columbus and torched most of the city's industries. Wilson was unaware that Robert E. Lee had surrendered at Appomattox one week earlier. The war was over. News of the surrender and Lincoln's assassination had not reached the deep south. Though there were outliers after – groups of people who refused to accept defeat – the Battle of Columbus is regarded by most historians to be the last land battle because neither side knew the war was over.

Lt. Col. John Stith Pemberton was severely injured in the battle. For years, he experimented with elixirs to ease his addiction to pain medicine, until he hit upon a recipe that would become Coca Cola. Though Atlanta often gets credit for Coke, because there it was manufactured and bottled, it was actually invented in Columbus. Pemberton's home is on the Columbus History Trail.

Pemberton is buried in Linwood Cemetery in Columbus, where Arthur Bussey, John Betjeman and Brig. Gen. Henry Benning are buried. Linwood Cemetery and the Columbus History Trail should be on your Fort Benning Bucket List.

William H. Parkman was David Richard's father. David's grandfather is also buried there. Joe Daniel Parkman, who was born in South Carolina in 1776, is buried near his son, William.

Main Post Cemetery

Dating to 1922, the Main Post Cemetery, on the east side of Benning Boulevard, is notable for its beauty and symmetry. Tombstones are all the same size and style, without regard to rank or position.

At the time of this writing, there are three Medal of Honor recipients buried in the Main Post Cemetery, including Spec. 4th Class Donald R. Johnston, who was the first MoH recipient to be buried on Fort Benning. The 22-year-old Columbus native was a mortarman, serving with the 1st Cavalry Division in the Tay Ninh Province on March 21, 1969, when he threw himself upon three enemy explosives to smother the blast and protect the six men he served alongside. Johnston was buried at the foot of the flagpole in the center of the cemetery, and I think you should make it a point to visit him at least once during your stay at Fort Benning.

Johnston   Schowalter   Nett

At the time of this writing, three Medal of Honor recipients are buried on Fort Benning.

You may also want to visit the graves of Col. Edward "Ned" Schowalter and Col. Robert Nett.

Schowalter was the second Medal of Honor recipient to be buried there in November 2003, one month shy of his 76th birthday. Schowalter joined the Merchant Marines at 17 during WWII, because he was too young for the Army. On October 14, 1952, the 25-year-old first lieutenant led his company in an attack on "Jane Russell Hill" near Kumhwa, Korea. He was knocked to the ground by an enemy slug to the head, which likely saved his life. Before he could recover, the Chinese dropped a basketful of grenades. Sprawled on the ground, Schowalter took a hit to his right side, but had he been standing, he said later, he would certainly have been killed. Refusing treatment and refusing to relinquish command, he stood and continued the fight, even after a third assault that broke his right arm. Schowalter also served two combat tours in Vietnam.

Robert Nett earned the Medal of Honor while fighting the Japanese in the Philippines in December 1944. He led a rifle and bayonet attack and single-handedly killed seven enemy soldiers. He was injured but refused medical treatment until his men reached the objective. Nett retired in Columbus and dedicated himself to mentoring officer candidates in his later years. Nett Hall on Fort Benning is one of several buildings named in his honor. He died at the age of 86 in October 2008.

Fun fact: Columbus is the only town in the country that can claim eight sons as Medal of Honor recipients, most of them having called Columbus home after they retired from the Army. You will find a memorial at the Eternal Flame at the Government Center on 10th Street in Columbus.

Also of note, Command Sgt. Maj. Eddie Crook Jr. was buried in the Main Post Cemetery in 2005. Crook served two tours in Vietnam and earned a Silver Star, a Bronze Star and two Purple Hearts. He also won an Olympic gold medal with Muhammad Ali in the 1960 Summer Olympics.

Fort Benning housed prison camps for Italian and German soldiers during WWII, and that is how seven Italian and 44 German prisoners came to rest in the Main Post Cemetery.

Italians are lovers, not fighters, and those imprisoned at Fort Benning during WWII were not altogether unhappy with their lot. They organized an orchestra to entertain the families on Fort Benning, and during the weekday, they were bussed off post to help harvest peanuts and cotton for local farmers whose sons were off fighting the war.

This 1943 photo shows Italian prisoners celebrating mass soon after learning of the end of hostilities between Italy and the Allies.

More than 2,900 Italian prisoners were detained at Fort Benning, and more than 90 percent of them participated in work details as part of the Italian Service Unit, organized by the Army. After Italy surrendered and joined the Allied war effort, the camp was cleared until German prisoners arrived in the spring of 1944.

Also buried in the Main Post Cemetery are Lt. Gen. Hal Moore and his wife, Julia.

The wives of 1st Cavalry Division at Fort Benning formed the Waiting Wives Club, a forerunner of the family readiness group, in November 1965, just over a month after the division shipped out to Vietnam. Led by Julia Moore, wife of (then) Lt. Col. Hal Moore, commander of the 7th Cav's 1st Battalion, the wives met at the Officers' Club after receiving news of the division's first death in

Vietnam. They offered strength and encouragement to one another, and together they campaigned for a change in the way families were notified of combat fatalities. Previously, they received telegrams delivered by local cab drivers. At the behest of the Waiting Wives Club, this practice ceased, and casualty notification teams were organized. After Julia Moore learned of the death of a first battalion soldier, Sgt. Jack Gell, while watching the news on TV, she called the post's Survivors Assistance Office and demanded they inform her of every 1st Battalion death thereafter. From that day forward, until her husband's unit returned, Moore never missed a local funeral or burial. Julia Moore died on April 18, 2004. She is buried in the Fort Benning Cemetery near her parents, Col. and Mrs. Louis Compton. Beside her lies Sgt. Jack Gell.

Hal and Julia Moore

Madeleine Stowe played the part of Julia Moore in the 2002 film *We Were Soldiers*. Mel Gibson played the part of her husband, Lt. Gen. Hal Moore, who was buried with his wife in 2017. The movie is based on the book written by Moore and Joe Galloway about the Battle of Ia Drang. Much of the movie was filmed at Fort Benning.

In the northeast corner of the Main Post Cemetery, near the outer brick wall, you'll find the graves of privates Curn Jones and John O'Conner, who were executed by hanging from a tree on Fort Benning in 1945. Jones and O'Conner had been taken prisoner after going AWOL and were forced to do manual labor every day. While working near the site of Russ Park, they ambushed the MP on guard duty and shot him to death with his gun. They eluded the MPs and made it to Harmony Church on foot, stole a Jeep, and made it as far as South Carolina before they were finally apprehended there.

Interment Form for Curn Jones

Curn and O'Conner were initially buried in unmarked graves outside the Main Post Cemetery, but their remains were relocated in 1983, and their graves were marked with headstones. On Memorial Day and Veterans Day, flags are traditionally placed on every grave in the cemetery, except for the graves of the only two soldiers ever formally executed on Fort Benning.

We do, on occasion (with less and less frequency) unearth the remains of Native American burial sites. In November 2011, utility workers installing an electric line under a parking lot on Main Post came across the ancient remains of at least four Native Americans estimated to be 2,000 or 3,000 years old, within the late Woodland to early Mississippian period. Among the relics unearthed was a gorget, a tribal neckpiece or necklace, indicating one person was likely a chief or a distinguished tribal leader of some kind. The gorget is extremely rare and in nearly pristine condition, making the remains significant to our Native American Tribal partners who preserved the remains for further study and reinterment. The National Historic Preservation Act of 1966 (which requires installations to notify tribes whenever remains or artifacts are found on federal property) and the 1992 Native American Graves and Repatriation Act guides Fort Benning's cooperative agreement with various tribal agencies.

CHAPTER 15:

Haunted Fort Benning

Most everyone enjoys a good ghost story, even those of us who don't believe. I present this information as straight news, just the way I received it from the people who shared their experiences with me. No need to embellish. I'll let you decide the veracity of these stories.

A sign on Richardson Circle marks the site of Kashita, the Creek Indian village you read about in Chapter 1. It tells of Col. John Tate, one of the last English agents sent to this area to muster up support for King George among the Lower Creeks during the years leading up to the Revolution. It is believed that Tate married Sehoya (or Sequoya, like the tree, depending on where you see it in print) the

Photo, circa 1920, shows a Military Police outpost (basically a checkpoint) near Main Post. Note the three ghostly figures in the roadway to the left of the MP.

daughter of a half chief. I don't even know what that means, but it reads well. About 1780, Tate fell ill and "died deranged between Flint River and Chattahoochee" enroute to Augusta with a party of Creeks, who lost heart for the battle and brought him back to Kashita for burial.

Some like to think he was buried on the grounds of what is now Riverside, the home of Fort Benning's commanding generals since 1919, but that's not likely. I have good reason to believe he was buried along the banks of the Upatoi River nearby. A map of Fort Benning in 1921 showed a cemetery near the river, and based upon historical context clues, historians believe it to be Tate's burial site. Maps created after the 1920s no longer included the cemetery, probably because cartographers saw no evidence of one. In the middle of the last century, as the post developed the land along Marne Road, construction workers unearthed bones. As was probably the practice more often than not, the workers reburied the bones and proceeded with the construction project. Though no written records exist today, the story has been handed down by employees who work in the facilities at the site, and there are those who claim to have experienced hauntings they attribute to the disturbance of the cemetery.

I first heard of Col. Tate in the fall of 2000, when my editor sent me looking for ghost stories on post. A young soldier who worked in Building 35, then the Western Hemisphere Institute for Security Cooperation (WHINSEC), told me he paid other soldiers to take his staff duty after being frightened one night by a ghost who haunted the halls during door check. He suggested I visit the library in the west wing of WHINSEC.

There I met the librarian who said the staff occasionally but not frequently saw a figure hanging out in the historical book section on warfare. I think that's hilarious. One of his staff members said the ghost rearranged chairs and moved stacks of books.

"But here's the thing that doesn't make sense," he said. "He wears a three-pointed hat and a cape and carries a saber. Fort Benning was built in 1919. At no point in Fort Benning history have soldiers dressed that way."

I called a friend who knew more about Fort Benning than most people. Her family roots were here, she lived on Fort Benning when her husband was assigned here, and she served as a docent at Riverside for many years.

"Well of course, everybody knows that's the ghost of Colonel John Tate," she said. "He loves to hang out at Building 35, but you'll find him mostly at Riverside. And you'll find him in old newspapers."

So I camped in the archives for several days. I discovered in the early 30s, the Fort Benning newspaper reported a growing concern among post residents who feared Main Post was haunted after various people reported seeing apparitions here and there, including one near Betjeman Bridge. Many speculated that the ghost was the victim of an automobile accident on or near the bridge several years earlier. Fort Benning wives were encouraged to "travel about the post in pairs," and residents were cautioned against picking up hitchhikers or accepting rides from strangers. Still pretty good advice, I think.

In October 1932, an article headlined "Phantom Rider Desires Automobiles," said MP squads reported seeing a "specter riding a big black charge down Benning Road toward Torch Hill." In recent weeks, the MPs said, the ghost was blamed for five automobile accidents. Presumably, the horseman was the ghost of Col. Tate, though contemporary accounts never include a horse.

The fact that the newspaper reported the accounts lent some credibility to the tales, but I suspect and cannot confirm the ghost stories were published for entertainment only with the assumption readers recognized them as such.

I mustered up the courage to call some of our former first wives and found three who were willing to go on record to attest to the existence of the late John Tate, though they didn't know him by name. One of the wives ran in the cool of the night when her husband was away, because it helped her sleep through the racket Tate made walking around the wooden veranda every night in his hobnailed boots. Another wife told me she put on her lipstick every morning in the mirror over the mantel, and every single day, the ghost hid her lipstick – in the same spot. Every. Single. Day.

That's the kind of strategy that lost them the war, I think.

A Sad, Sweet Spirit

Col. Tate isn't the only ghost who haunts Riverside. It was one of the wives of a post commander who first told me she knew she shared her home with the "gentle, friendly spirit of a young girl." I'm confident her friend is the ghost of Barbara King, who was 23 years old when she died.

Barbara was the daughter of Maj. Gen. Campbell King, who commanded Fort Benning from 1929-1933. When the general discovered Barbara was carrying on a relationship with his driver, an enlisted man, he had the young man reassigned, and it broke his daughter's heart.

Barbara's dad would hang his holster on the stair post while he took a 30-minute nap at noon every day, and soon after he separated Barbara from her love, she took his pistol from the stair post and laid down in the bedroom next to his and put the gun to her heart. The post newspaper offered front-page condolences to the General and Mrs. Campbell over their daughter's death due to "sudden and unexpected illness" in January of 1933. I truly hate this story.

The Columbus newspaper listed Barbara King as 21 years old and reported her death as the result of the flu. Neither was correct.

Though Barbara was buried at Arlington National Cemetery, former residents say her sweet, gentle spirit has not left Riverside. Two of the former first ladies said they knew, intuitively, that the spirit was a young female. She did, however, cause a fury one Christmas morning, when she started flinging packages from under the tree. The family left to spend the day elsewhere.

I think Maj. Gen. King had no business meddling in his daughter's personal affairs, since he was married to his first cousin. For Pete's sake.

Barbara's death certificate belied reports she died after a sudden illness.

Oh Baby, a Ghost in the House

If Riverside is the most haunted house on Fort Benning, a home on Baltzell Avenue surely comes in a close second. Residents have experienced the kinds of odd occurrences one would associate with hauntings, including cold spots, the sounds of a child playing when there were no children in the house, the sound of someone playing a harmonica in the middle of the night, and the cat staring at something that appeared to be nothing. The "little girl ghost" was friendly, but occasionally mischievous, hiding toys and turning electronics on and off.

When asked to leave "for a while," the little girl complied, but she returned when the family added a new baby, and she brought a friend with her. The newest guest dressed as one would expect a nanny or nurse to have dressed in the latter part of the nineteenth century, before Fort Benning existed. The lady who lived there when the new ghost moved in believed the birth of her son had stirred up the spirit of a governess who had lived near the house, perhaps the governess who had once cared for the little girl ghost. The new ghost seemed protective of the baby, and she picked him up out of his crib once when he was much too young to climb out and put him down on the floor of his nursery, where his mother found him playing happily with someone who wasn't there.

The family hosted a gathering at their house, a come-one-come-all type of affair, and as is often the case in military circles, friends brought friends. At the end of the evening, a woman – a stranger to the family – approached the hostess on her way out the door, and left with these words: "You know you have a spirit, don't you? She means you no harm. She just came to look after the baby."

A Spirited Ghost

I interviewed four people who lived on the same street on Main Post at different times, including two local women who were teenagers when their fathers served on Fort Benning in the 1970s and 80s, and two women who lived in the same haunted house just a few years apart and very recently. Four women, four decades, and all in agreement.

In the 70s and early 80s, families in the neighborhood understood there were three houses in a row that were visited by the spirit of a soldier dressed in olive drab from head to toe. He knocked on doors, rang the doorbells, and occasionally allowed himself to be seen. Now grown with children of their own, two Columbus residents told me they were teenagers when they lived near those houses, and it was generally accepted by everyone in the neighborhood, adults and kids alike, that those three houses were haunted.

In more contemporary reports, he stays home and only occasionally ventures out to explore the neighborhood. Someone who lived there about 10 years ago said it took a while to figure out they "weren't being pranked by neighbor kids" when the doorbell rang repeatedly – day after day – after the family settled into bed each night.

A former post resident named Deanna reached out to me to share her story after reading my Haunted Fort Benning series on social media several years ago. In her words, edited for brevity:

"We had quite a few strange things happen that I just dismissed or ignored early on, but we could never actually explain them.

My husband moved in a couple of weeks before me, and later he told me he'd heard voices, as if there were people talking somewhere in the house. When he was in the basement, he said, he was never alone, and someone or something turned the lights on down there. He blamed it all on the age of the house, the air ducts, the wiring or vents or whatever, so he didn't tell me about it at first because he didn't want me to freak out.

My experiences started shortly after my son and I moved in. One night at 10 p.m., we were awakened by a loud crash just outside our bedroom door. A very large, framed painting had fallen off the wall at the end of the hall. Again, nothing to be concerned about, it could have easily happened. It wasn't until it happened again and again, several times to several different pictures in different locations and always at 10 p.m. that we realized something wasn't right.

Shortly after that, our doorbell started ringing in the middle of the night for no reason. I guess our ghost had a sense of humor, because one time when I was telling my mother-in-law about the pictures and the doorbell ringing at night, the doorbell rang. Again, no one was there. I guess he just wanted to corroborate my story. I appreciated that, you know, because it was my mother-in-law.

One evening, when I was cooking dinner, I called to my son to come eat just as I was reaching into a cabinet, and I saw a hand come up over my shoulder by my neck. I thought it was my son teasing me, but I turned and he wasn't there. I ran from the kitchen through the dining room, across the hall to the living room, thinking I was chasing my son.

That's when I saw him coming downstairs.

I stood there in shock and blurted out what had just happened. Instead of thinking his mom was crazy, he told me his story. He came home from school one day and heard someone walking around upstairs. He looked out the window to see whose car was in the driveway, mine or my husband's. Neither. We weren't home.

Finally, just before we moved again, I was in the kitchen again when I caught a very brief glimpse of what appeared to be a young man, slim, and dressed in tan or khaki. He was there, but he wasn't, and it happened so fast. That's the last we saw or heard of him."

And that's the last I heard of him, too, until very recently, when having coffee with a friend who lives near Deanna's former house. My friend described a ghost fitting the same description who showed up late one night when she was alone watching television.

"He looked as startled as I felt," she said. "I don't think he expected to see me any more than I expected to see him. And then he was gone, just like that."

CHAPTER 16

Remembering Felix Hall

It's a different kind of ghost that haunts us over the death of Pvt. Felix Hall. In the spring of 1941, the body of a young black soldier was found hanging in a shallow ravine in the woods to the west of Fort Benning's Main Post. The hot Georgia sun and maggots had done unthinkable things to his body and challenged investigators' ability to make sense of the crime scene early on. But the baling wire used to bind his hands and feet was all the evidence needed to refute post officials' decision to declare his death suicide.

It took several weeks and a national public outcry to gin up enough interest within the War Department and the FBI to launch an investigation. I'm not sure if it was a case of too little, too late, or if

In 2022, a marker was erected on the spot near Main Post where Felix Hall was found hanging in 1941.

there simply wasn't enough evidence to convict any one of the three men identified as suspects. The investigation was hampered by lack of cooperation among white soldiers and fear of cooperation among black soldiers.

Less than six months after his body was discovered, the Japanese bombed Pearl Harbor and launched the United States into war, and interest in the horrific murder petered out. In what was believed to be the only lynching on a federal installation in U.S. history, the murder of 19-year-old Pvt. Felix Hall has never been solved.

It's likely anyone and everyone who might have known who killed Felix has since died.

Sadly, no one knows where he's buried – perhaps in an unmarked grave back in Millbrook, Alabama, where he was left after his mother's death to be raised by his grandmother. The only work available to black teenagers in Millbrook was field labor, so six months before his death, at the age of 18, Felix enlisted in the Army.

In 2021, Fort Benning erected a memorial marker on the spot where Pvt. Hall was last seen alive, walking from the sawmill where he worked toward the area where 24th Infantry Regiment soldiers were segregated outside of the workday.

I'm grateful for an Army confronting its past, but for Felix Hall it's too late, and we can never change that. He was just a boy. I wish we didn't have to dedicate memorials to 19-year-old boys who take the wrong way home.

CHAPTER 17

An Odd and Interesting Time

The 1940s was an odd and interesting decade on Fort Benning, largely because of the war. Here is an abbreviated list of notable anecdotes that made the news:

• As part of the war conservation efforts, a senior commander's wife encouraged Fort Benning wives to feed their babies the "old fashioned way … as nursing one's baby is a natural act and it has been known to give a deep sense of maternal satisfaction."

• Post residents were not permitted to host guests overnight without prior written consent from garrison officials. Unauthorized guests would be picked up by the military police and escorted off post. Seems harsh.

• Troops assigned to the Women's Army Auxiliary Corps begin arriving on Fort Benning to replace male soldiers in nonmilitary assignments, such as clerical jobs and service jobs at the clubs on post. The newspaper ran a gently misogynistic reminder prior to their arrival that the first WAAC on Fort Benning was actually a dog, a female of course, the mascot of the 283 Quartermaster Refrigeration Company. Her name was WAAC.

• As a reward for having the best mess hall on post, the personnel of the First Student Training Regiment mess hall were each given a carton of cigarettes and a five-dollar bill.

• When a popular dining establishment in Columbus was short-staffed, Fort Benning soldiers went to work peeling potatoes. "To the kitchen they went and put their KP experience to good advantage."

• 508 1st Division Road was the residence of Mrs. James Notestein, who hosted the first meeting of the Women's Club's

Victory Garden Group. With permission from the post commander to use land traditionally reserved for flower gardens, the Victory Garden Group would join the wartime conservation efforts by growing (and sharing) their own vegetables.

• In February of 1943, the post newspaper reported "Max is rarin' to go" according to an official from the 505th Parachute

Regiment. Max was a 70-pound Boxer, a 'parapup' with eight airborne jumps to his credit. On the morning he was scheduled to make number nine, Max was hit by a truck and suffered extensive injuries. Upon his release from the Veterinary Hospital, Max was deemed fit for service, promoted to master sergeant, and awarded a "wound stripe" for suffering an injury in the line of duty.

• Fort Benning officials announced that soldiers would be issued khaki underwear, since white underwear presented "a danger on the battlefield because they could be easily seen by enemy bombers when hung out to dry in combat zones."

• Officials released a list of new measures that would be employed to enhance conservation efforts on post in support of the war, including the assignment of a civilian whose job it would be to "watch the moon" and note when it was bright enough to turn off the streetlights.

CHAPTER 18

Murder on Main Post

There have been several murders on Fort Benning, but none more salacious than the murder of Elizabeth "Betty" Brooke, who was bludgeoned to death by her husband on June 8, 1938, while their children were locked out of their home on Main Post.

Maj. John Rutter Brooke Jr. was a tactical instructor at the Infantry School, a heavy-set former football player with a cynical smile and a gambling addiction that led to the financial problems that likely led to Betty's death. Prosecutors believed Brooke anticipated an insurance payout that would alleviate his debt.

John sent the couple's three children outside to play, two daughters and a son named John Rutter III, who was born at the Fort Benning Station Hospital in 1929. Twice they tried to enter the house, and twice their father refused them admission. The second time, he went so far as to push his daughter out of a window, she told authorities.

John proclaimed his innocence in the matter of his wife's murder and defended his behavior with the claim that he and his wife were "having relations" on the davenport in the living room, and they didn't want the children to disturb them.

Betty, a former nurse who married Brooke soon after his first wife drowned in a boating accident while alone with her husband, had made plans to run errands with a friend the morning of June 8th. Betty's friend testified that she became worried after her phone calls went unanswered and drove to the Brooke house, where she found the doors locked and the curtains drawn over the windows on what was an oppressively hot day.

John Brooke and his family lived in this house on Main Post before he murdered his wife in what appeared to be a sloppy attempt to claim her life insurance.

Before noon, a neighbor saw John leave in the family car carrying what appeared to be a bundle of clothing, and shortly thereafter, he reported for field maneuvers in a training area several miles from Main Post off Ochillee Road. Fellow officers expressed surprise at seeing Brooke in the field on what was supposed to be his day off.

When the Brooke children came home for lunch, they found their mother's body crumpled at the bottom of the stairway near the front door, her hand clutching the bloody wound on her head. A child's golf club, a mid-iron, was found next to her lifeless body. A trail of blood led to the couple's bedroom upstairs.

Investigators immediately suspected the husband, who showed no sign of distress or grief when he was led to the morgue to identify his wife that afternoon.

Fate is fickle. Though it did poor Betty no favors on the morning of her death, it favored her in the afternoon, when an unsuspecting soldier collecting figs with his children off McBride Road happened upon a bloody khaki shirt lying on the ground beneath a fig tree. A laundry label identified the shirt as belonging to John Brooke. Trousers were found in a ditch nearby.

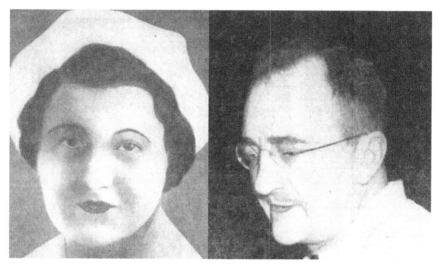

Betty and John Brooke

During a two-week trial in September, the post commander, Maj. Gen. Asa Singleton, testified on the stand to Brooke's good character, but the defendant did little to help his own cause. He was snarky and combative, wagging his finger at the prosecutor and responding to questions with questions of his own.

Why not take your lovemaking upstairs and lock the bedroom door, the prosecutor asked. Why lock the children out of the house?

"Why do you do a lot of things?" Brooke replied with a dismissive shrug.

The jury found him guilty of first-degree murder, and he was sentenced to life in prison.

John Rutter Brooke was a fourth-generation soldier. His great grandfather, Maj. William Brooke, fought in the War of 1812. His grandfather and namesake, Maj. Gen. John Rutter Sr., led Union troops at Antietam and Gettysburg, fought in the Spanish-American War, and is buried at Arlington National Cemetery. Brooke Avenue in Gettysburg is named in his honor. The major general's son, the murderer's father, Col. William Brooke, is buried in Fort Sam Houston National Cemetery near his grandson, John Brooke III, who served in the Navy during the Korean War.

John Rutter Brooke Jr. is buried in a civilian cemetery in Texas under his mother's maiden name with no indication or acknowledgement of his service.

Today, this entrance is often referred to as the Stone Gate, and it serves as the inbound lane on Fort Benning Road that leads past the National Infantry Museum to Main Post. For more than 50 years, this was the primary route for soldiers traveling to post from Columbus. Picture circa 1950.

CHAPTER 19

Believe It or Not

Legend has it that Fort Benning made history in the 1940s with various inclusions in *Ripley's Believe It or Not!*

According to *Ripley's*, The Infantry Center Chapel was notable for "serving the most faiths" of any church in the country. It was said to have served five faiths in the 1940s, and I have no idea what those included.

The Three Faiths Chapel (TIC Chapel) is pictured here during construction in 1925. It would quickly outgrow its original purpose to accommodate services for Catholic, Protestant, and Jewish faiths.

The Infantry Center Chapel is commonly referred to as the TIC Chapel. When it was dedicated in November of 1934, it was called the Three Faiths Chapel and it accommodated services for the post's Catholic, Protestant and Jewish communities. By the 1940s, it had outgrown those three congregations. It was funded with that same Depression-era public works money that gave us Building 35 and the Officers' Club, or "O Club." The O Club was renamed Benning Club when the post club system became more inclusive, and it will soon become Club 1918 to commemorate the founding of the installation.

The Infantry Center Chapel

The design of the chapel is noted for its understated elegance and 100-foot-tall steeple. The original carillon was donated to the Army by the family of Harvey Firestone Jr. as a tribute to the American soldiers who died in WWI. (Firestone served as an aviator in WWI. You might be driving around on his tires.) The carillon was presented to Fort Benning in 1946, and for many years, folks would drive from Columbus and surrounding communities to enjoy the 30-minute carillon concert that started at 5 p.m. each day.

Ripley's also reported the single contiguous Cuartel had the world's longest porch in 1941. The Cuartels are those massive red-brick barracks complexes between Vibbert and Wold on the northwest corner of Main Post. "Cuartels" is the Spanish word for barracks. These were built between 1925 and 1929 during the post's first major construction period, making them the oldest barracks on post. That period was distinguished by heavy Spanish influence in architecture.

This circa 1925 photo shows the construction of the single continuous cuartel in the background. The cuartels, or barracks (in Spanish), would eventually replace the wooden structures in the foreground.

And finally, Fort Benning was said to have the world's longest narrow-gauge railroad. More on that in Chapter 20.

Legend or lie? I've never been able to find proof that Fort Benning was mentioned in *Ripley's*, but I suspect there is a grain of truth in it, as there is in most legends and tall tales. Because *Ripley's* was originally a newspaper panel, similar to a comic strip, and was later adapted into a wide variety of formats, including radio, television and comic books, before it became the book series we're most familiar with today, it's quite possible (even probable, given the random and niche nature of the claims) that someone set out to get Fort Benning in the record books and did so successfully, even if the "record books" turned out to be a mere mention on the radio.

A narrow railway is one that has less than the standard railroad gauge of 4 feet, 8.5 inches.

Soon after Arthur Bussey built Riverside in 1909, he devised a method to pump water up the hill from a nearby spring to cool his dairy. Ten years later, the spring was dammed to create a pond. Today, the two bodies of water, Russ Pond and Russ Pool, are the centerpiece of Russ Park, located on the north side of Main Post.

Though the pond and pool were used for combat water training and swim competitions, it was also said to be the most popular swimming spot in the Chattahoochee Valley well into the midcentury. In 1926, the park included a beach and concrete stands with seating for 400. A bathhouse was added soon after, and the post newspaper told ladies they could use the automatic hairdryer by depositing one nickel!

The pool eventually fell into disrepair when the cost of maintenance and repair became prohibitive, but the site remains popular with Fort Benning families, who enjoy fishing, picnic pavilions, a disc golf course, playgrounds, and a fitness trail. Fishing at Russ Park is reserved for family members 15 and younger.

CHAPTER 20

The Dinky Line

Fort Benning had its own narrow-gauge railroad from 1921 to 1946.

The locomotives were built for use in World War I by the Davenport Locomotive Works of Iowa. After the war, it was shipped to Camp Benning to be used in construction projects around post, but it was also used to taxi soldiers to and from various training areas and "classrooms in the field". When it was deemed to have served its purpose, it was dismantled and sold to a sugar plantation in Cuba. Truly random, right?

Soldiers called the train Dinky Line, Chattahoochee Choo-Choo, and Old Fuss and Feathers. At the height of its use, there were more

The Dinky Line was used to carry construction materials around the new post.

than 18 locomotives and 27 miles of track that was narrower than the standard 4-foot 8.5-inch track. It had 32 coaches, 53 flat cars, 105 gondolas, four tank cars, 10 locomotives and a special observation car built in 1935 for visiting dignitaries. Engine No. 1902 and the VIP car are all that remains of the Dinky Line; you will see them on display at the National Infantry Museum.

The post newspaper reported in February 1927 that Pvt. Joseph Wiggins saved the life of Sgt. Frank Lavender's 18-month-old baby, who had ventured through a hole in the screen door of the family home and toddled onto the train tracks.

"Wiggins, at the throttle of the post's narrow-gauge train, noticed an infant crawling on the tracks ahead and immediately applied the brakes," the article said. "Because of the angle of the grade, the train would not stop. Wiggins jumped out and ran ahead of the train to snatch the baby just in the nick of time."

Lavender tried to talk to Wiggins, who hopped back on the train. The private later explained, "I didn't have time to answer any d--- fool questions. I had to get that load of sand and gravel out where I was going."

From the File Marked No Kidding

In March 1943, post officials invited officials from Phenix City to a Victory Luncheon to celebrate a milestone; for a period of one month, not a single case of venereal disease on Fort Benning could be traced back to Phenix City, Alabama. That was a mark of success in what was being called the Venereal Battle after 40,000-man hours had been lost in 1942 to a sexually transmitted disease. The soldier in charge of leading the battle? His name was Maj. Loveless!

If you know nothing about the colorful history of Phenix City and the relationship between the town and the post, I highly recommend the book *The Phenix City Story*.

CHAPTER 21

Leonard Nimoy Slept Here

An awful lot of famous people have passed this way. Some stayed a while, but most didn't.

Jazz legend Louis Armstrong was among the first. He performed for the troops on Fort Benning on Christmas Day in 1942.

Norman Rockwell spent just enough time on Fort Benning in 1943 to create a series of sketches called A Night on a Troop Train with the Paratroopers. *The Saturday Evening Post* feature depicted soldiers in various stages of preparation for deployment.

Then came Jane Russell. The actress and pin-up model boarded in Columbus and lent her star power to raise funds for the war

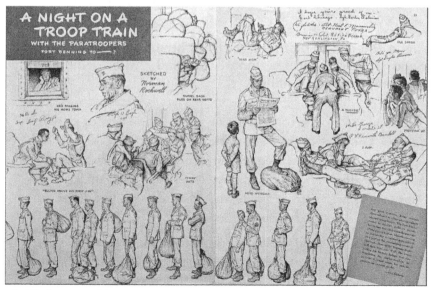

A Night on a Troop Train was illustrated by Norman Rockwell after his visit to Fort Benning.

effort while her husband attended Officer Candidate School at Fort Benning from 1943 to 1944. The post newspaper published a photo spread that showed Russell sweeping and pouring coffee for her husband, who could only visit her in Columbus on weekends, under the headline "Pin-Up Girl Jane Russell Is Typical Benning Wife."

Jane Russell is pictured with her husband, Bob Waterfield, who played professional football when his Army commitment was fulfilled.

"Jane may not be so well-known to the uninitiated civilian, but to every G.I. she's a barracks institution," the article said. "Just ask your bunkmate to show you whose picture adorns the inside of his footlocker. Ten to one its Jane Russell in one of her familiar poses. And fellows, take it from a G.I. who went, saw and was conquered. She's a honey and her pictures don't lie."

Russell's husband, Bob Waterfield, was a standout for the UCLA Bruins before joining the Army. He played for the 176th Infantry team at Fort Benning and went on to play for the Rams after he was discharged and was inducted into the Pro Football Hall of Fame in 1965.

Lewis Grizzard was born at Martin Army Hospital in 1946, but he didn't stay long. Alan Alda, Leonard Nimoy and James Earl Jones all stayed for a while. The three of them were stationed at Benning. Nimoy, who was assigned to the Army's Special Services branch, wrote and emceed shows and appeared in training films before he was discharged in 1955 as a technician third class, the equivalent to a staff sergeant.

Tech Third Class Nimoy

Dave Thomas, the founder of Wendy's, attended Cooks and Bakers School during the Korean War. He attributed his success to his training here.

Bob Hope dropped by for a visit in 1972, but he didn't film here. He came to Fort Benning to help raise funds to build a new Infantry Museum. He spoke at a benefit in Columbus and dropped in for an afternoon tea at the Fort Benning Officers' Club, where he was hailed an honorary member of the Officers' Wives Club.

Bob Hope at Fort Benning in 1972

They also presented him a pair of Infantry blue slippers with the motto "Follow Me" embroidered on them. When the president of the OWC proposed a toast to Hope and 500 women raised their glasses, Hope was heard to mutter, "Please don't throw 'em."

(The "new" museum was never built on post; it took up residence in the former Station Hospital on Baltzell Avenue, the present site of the Western Hemisphere Institute for Security Cooperation, until the National Infantry Museum was built on Benning Road in 2009.)

Jimmy Stewart, the actor, did not serve on Fort Benning, though he did enlist and serve as an aviator in WWII. Fort Benning's Stewart Field is actually named for Staff Sgt. Jimmy Stewart, who gave his life and earned the Medal of Honor in Vietnam.

Fort Benning is comprised of 182,000 acres, and 20,000 of them are in Alabama, where you will find the Uchee Creek Campground, a resort and recreation center that should be on your Fort Benning Bucket List. Uchee Creek is only seven miles from Main Post but worlds away.

The *other* Jimmy Stewart

When John Wayne came to Fort Benning in 1967 to film the iconic war movie *The Green Berets*, much of the filming took place in the vicinity of Uchee Creek, where set designers transformed Alabama wilderness into jungles, outposts and villages, a set design so realistic, Fort Benning used them afterward to train soldiers destined for Vietnam.

John Wayne is pictured at the Benning Supper Club on the Set of *The Green Berets*. Photo: Alabama Department of Archives and History. Donated by Alabama Media Group. Photo by Tom Self, Birmingham News.

Wayne, always a supporter of the military, said he made this movie to counter the growing anti-war sentiment. He turned down the role of Maj. Reisman in *The Dirty Dozen* to direct and star in *The Green Berets*, which premiered at Fort Benning on July 4, 1968.

Post historians have tried with little success to locate the areas near Uchee Creek, such as the one below, that were used during the filming of *The Green Berets*.

Most of the film was shot on post, which explains a few of the technical errors, including the fact that the sun set in the wrong horizon. Fort Benning also served as the backdrop for scenes that were supposed to take place at Fort Bragg. Scenes were filmed at Lawson Army Airfield and the Benning Supper Club, which was brand spanking new at the time.

This set from *The Green Berets* was located near Uchee Creek.

Anti-war critics hated the movie – Roger Ebert gave it zero stars – but audiences loved it. The film became one of John Wayne's biggest box-office successes, grossing nearly $22 million. "The left-wingers are shredding my flesh, but we're bawling all the way to the bank," Wayne said.

The Green Berets is perhaps the most notable movie filmed at Fort Benning, but there have been several that were marginally successful, including, most recently, *We Were Soldiers*, the Vietnam movie starring Mel Gibson as Lt Col. Hal Moore and Sam Elliot as Command Sgt Maj. Basil Plumley.

Parachute Battalion was filmed at Fort Benning in 1941, when the concept was still new to the American audience. The movie starred Buddy Ebson, best known for his work in *The Beverly Hillbillies* and *Barnaby Jones*. The opening film credits, "We gratefully acknowledge the splendid cooperation given by the officers and men of the 501st Parachute Battalion at Fort Benning, Georgia, who actually made all the parachute jumps in this picture."

Dean Martin and Jerry Lewis filmed *Jumping Jacks* at Fort Benning in 1951; James Garner filmed *Tank* in 1984; and Barbara Eden, of *I Dream of Jeannie* fame, filmed *Your Mother Wears Combat Boots* here in 1989.

It's fun to share stories about celebrities who passed this way, but I could write chapters about the Very Important People, the leaders and warriors and heroes who made their home on Fort Benning for a time. Sometimes, when their names are Patton or Eisenhower or Powell, we put a brass marker on the door of the house they called home, and they remain in the post inventory of residential quarters. Fortunate are the families who get to live in those houses, I think.

The house that served as the home of the Moore family in the filming of the movie *We Were Soldiers* is located on the back of Miller Loop. Hal and Julia Moore never lived on Miller Loop; they lived a couple of blocks over on Austin Loop. However, while the movie was being filmed in 2002, their son, who was an officer assigned to Fort Benning, lived just down the street at the end of Miller Loop, where he could step out onto his porch and watch filming take place just down the block.

Gen. George Patton was a colonel when he arrived at Fort Benning in 1940, and here he earned his first and second stars. It was at Fort Benning that he was given the nickname "Old Blood N' Guts" after repeatedly warning his troops about the macabre nature of war.

He commanded the 2nd Armored Division on Sand Hill and led the division on a 400-mile march from Columbus to Panama City, Florida, and back. Patton and his wife Beatrice lived on Baltzell Avenue for a time before moving out to a home on Sand Hill, a home some people say he built for himself. It's more likely he simply had the clout to make the Army build the new house, so he could be closer to his troops, but it is certainly true that he could have funded the construction. Patton was independently wealthy, so much so that Gen. Omar Bradley once called him "the richest man in the Army". Legend has it, and I cannot prove, that he gave his paycheck to the agency we now call the Army Emergency Relief Fund to help soldiers in need. When he left Fort Benning, he turned in the keys to that house on Sand Hill and it served as a clubhouse until it burned in the 1960s.

Three homes were recently dedicated as part of the new(ish) Black History Trail, including the quarters of First Sgt. Walter Morris on Meehan Street and First Lt. Benjamin O. Davis Jr. You read about them in Chapter 13. The late Gen. Colin Powell lived on Arrowhead Road from 1964 to 1967 when he was promoted from captain to major upon his return from Vietnam.

Truth be told, we rub elbows with more real heroes every time we go to the commissary than most people will every meet in their lifetime. If we turned every hero's home into a museum, there would be no homes available for residency.

In the 1930s, we measured funny by the feet. More than 1,700 patrons squeezed into the 1,200-seat Main Post Theater in January of 1930 to see (and hear!) a talking picture for the first time. Adults paid a quarter and kids paid a dime to movies that were measured in miles and feet. The Infantry School News published a list of great movies showing at the Main Post Theater, including The Night Club – "Six reels, one mile and 450 feet of good comedy!" Fort Benning was the first of 85 Army theaters to install sound equipment for talking picture shows.

CHAPTER 22

Benning on the Bay

Thank heaven for slow-growing oaks.

In the early 1800s, President John Quincy Adams set aside 30,000 acres in the Florida panhandle to establish an oak preserve. A few longleaf pines were thrown in for good measure. It was the nation's first commercial forestry project, and one that proved disappointing. Mature oaks wouldn't be harvested until just prior to the Civil War.

So in 1842, part of the land was deeded to the military, and the Moreno Point Military Reservation was established to produce tar, pitch and turpentine from those pines for use by the military.

Shortly thereafter, about 1845, a fisherman named Leonard Destin sailed from Connecticut and dropped anchor at the mouth of

Fort Benning Soldiers are pictured at the Infantry Center Rest Camp in Destin, Florida.

Choctawhatchee Bay. He was probably seeking shelter from a storm, but he liked what he found there well enough to stay. Destin built a cabin and set up a commercial fishing operation. A settlement grew up around him, comprised solely of settlers involved in the fishing industry, who built their homes on the government land attached to the Moreno Point Military Reservation. Their settlement became known as Destin.

When the Depression hit hard in the 1930s and the military closed shop at Moreno Point, the Army sold the settlers the land they were living on. Whatever land was left was put up for auction.

Maj. Franklin Sibert bought some of the land to build a vacation home for his family. The Fort Benning soldier suggested to the Infantry Board that a camp be established in Destin for post personnel. In 1935, two lots, about 12 acres, were withdrawn from the sale and put under the jurisdiction of the commandant of the Infantry School to be used as a campsite and recreational area for the Fort Benning community. It was called the Infantry Center Rest Camp.

Pictured is a cabin at the Rest Camp in its infancy. Today, the resort offers a variety of lodging, including villas and an RV park.

Sibert, a battalion commander of the 29th Infantry Regiment, took charge of construction there. By September 1936, six wood-frame cottages had been built, at a cost of $1,500, on 1,000 feet of bayside beach frontage. Guests would find hammocks, horseshoes and one aluminum rowboat at their disposal. Water and sewer lines were added nearly 20 years later, and a couple of new guest quarters were constructed from concrete block.

In the 60s and 70s, the Destin Army Recreation Area grew and grew. Cabins were added, and a snack bar, marina and boathouse were built. An RV campground and bath house were built in 1982.

These days, Sibert wouldn't recognize his legacy. Neither would Destin, for that matter. Just as the city has grown to a bustling tourist mecca, Fort Benning's premier recreation center — now more than 15 acres — has grown to include a swimming pool and splash pad, a motel, efficiency apartments and a number of contemporary cabins, or 'villas.' Guests enjoy bayside access to the gulf, deep-sea fishing and dolphin sighting tours.

The Destin Army Recreation Center is nestled inside a gated resort in the heart of Destin, just minutes from Panama City, Fort Walton Beach, Eglin Air Force Base and a pristine strip of gulf-side beach owned by Eglin and reserved for the military. The rec center should be on your Fort Benning Bucket List. Google it.

On March 7, 1945, US forces captured the Ludendorff Bridge during a prolonged battle between American and German forces near the town of Remagen, allowing Allied Forces to cross the River Rhine in great numbers for the first time. The Germans tried repeatedly to destroy the bridge. It finally collapsed 10 days later, too late to stem the flow of Allied forces across the river, the Nazis' last natural line of defense against Western forces. Six stones from the bridge were used to form the base of the American Infantryman Statue that stands in the park facing Edwards Street on Fort Benning's Main Post. Staff Sgt. Thomas E. Love modeled for this statue, a replica of a statue that stands in Berlin, Germany. It was unveiled at Fort Benning in 1958.

CHAPTER 23

Don't Call Him Mike

It's a 4,000-pound sculpture with a monumental identity crisis.

The statue that stands in front of post headquarters is not The Follow Me Statue. The fine looking fellow atop the massive stone foundation is not Iron Mike. He was named the Infantryman when he was erected on Eubanks Field in 1960, which was potentially, if only mildly, problematic, because The American Infantryman Statue stood a few blocks to the east in front of Building 35, which was the post headquarters at that time.

When President Gerald Ford visited Fort Benning on June 14, 1975, to celebrate the Army's bicentennial birthday, he spoke to a crowd of 25,000 gathered on York Field in front of Building 4 (then

The Infantryman, or Follow Me Statue, originally stood on Eubanks Field.

Infantry Hall, now McGinnis-Wickam Hall) where the Infantryman had been relocated several years earlier, soon after the new post headquarters were opened. Ford referred to the Infantryman as "the Follow Me Statue".

The name is entirely appropriate given the posture of the figure in the classic "follow me" pose, "Follow Me!" being the Army Infantry motto.

Call him what you like – the Infantryman or Follow Me – just don't call him Mike. Iron Mike is The Airborne Trooper, and his home is Fort Bragg. He's an ally.

In 2004, the statue of an Infantryman not named Mike was shipped off to Loveland, Colorado for repair, and a duplicate was made. The original statue became part of the National Infantry Museum collection and sits on a granite pedestal in the rotunda outside the museum. The duplicate now shares the spotlight in front of post headquarters with the Armor School's Trooper of the Plains.

Who is the Infantryman?

The story of the Follow Me Statue is fun and fabulous from start to finish, but nothing impresses me more than the fact that it was sculpted by two soldiers, Pvt. First Class Manfred Bass, the sculptor and designer, and his assistant Pvt. First Class Karl H. Van Krog. Bass went on to serve as the chief designer for Macy's Parade Studio for more than 40 years.

Fort Benning's commanding general, Maj. Gen. Paul Freeman, commissioned the statue in 1959, and he selected a 26-year-old officer candidate and Korean War veteran Maj. Eugene Wyles from a pool of potential models.

When I interviewed Wyles in 2004, he told me Maj. Gen. Freeman said he had been chosen because he was "grizzly." He had a rugged build and a chiseled jawline, both characteristics Wyles attributed to his native American heritage. Wyles also said Freeman originally planned to name the statue "the Ultimate Infantryman".

Wyles was 17 years old, the son of a sharecropper, when he joined the Army in 1950 and shipped off to Korea. He enjoyed the challenge of Army life and made rank right on schedule. When he hit a glass ceiling in his military occupational specialty some eight or nine years later, he decided to attend Officer Candidate School. That's where Maj. Gen. Paul Freeman recruited him to model.

The Fort Benning commander commissioned two soldiers to design and sculpt the Infantryman Statue in 1959.

The rest is history, they say, but the truth is, history is a natural editor, and much of Wyles' military record remains obscure. I found it in faded news accounts and a dog-eared scrapbook put together by one of Wyles' fans. Wyles served two tours in Vietnam, including a stint as an advisor to a remote village. There he received a call from his commander one night. A nearby village was surrounded by Viet

Cong and in danger of being overrun. Wyles was ordered to lead a contingent of soldiers into the village and stave off the attack, which he did. He called in firepower all night long, and come dawn, reinforcements arrived.

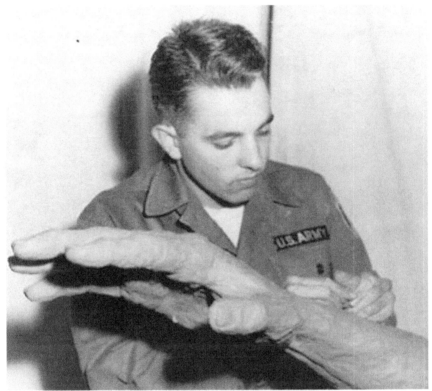

Pvt. First Class Manfred Bass sculpting The Infantryman.

Success came with a heavy price.

"I was feeling quite proud of myself," he recalled. "Then they started bringing in the dead children. It changed me. We did what we had to do, but nobody wants to see innocent children die."

Wyles remained in the village for six months, during which he spearheaded a toy drive back in the states. Weekly shipments of toys and clothes were delivered to the Vietnamese children.

When he returned to the states, Wyles started a youth camp for orphaned Native Americans on a reservation in Montana. He raised three of his own and nearly half a dozen foster children.

He was a gifted songwriter and musician and some of his early work, mostly war related Vietnam-era ballads, garnered national attention, even an invitation to appear on the Ed Sullivan Show. Later, he performed in Louisiana with The Swamp Gang, a regional country-western band that frequently performed benefit concerts. When I spoke to him, he was making plans to help a local retired police officer who lost his leg to diabetes.

Retired Maj. Eugene Wyles returned to Fort Benning to celebrate the 50th anniversary of the dedication of the statue.

Freeman died in 2010 at the age of 77.

I dare say Maj. Gen. Freeman could not have known how appropriate his choice was when he selected young Wyles to model for the Follow Me Statue. The battle-scarred, grizzly Infantryman epitomized the kind of selfless service characteristic of a model American soldier.

In 1937, Capt. Robert Howie and Master Sgt. Melvin Wiley built a machine gun carrier from spare automobile parts they retrieved from the scrap heap at Fort Benning. Assistant Commandant Walter Short invited an engineer from Willys-Overland Motors to see a demonstration of the vehicle. He recognized its potential and took the first step toward the development of the Jeep. Willys-Overland produced 360,000 Jeeps by 1945.

CHAPTER 24

A Horsie Post

From the outset, the Fort Benning community was known for its love of horses. Soldiers and family members took classes in equitation, horse shows drew crowds from far and wide, and polo was the most popular sport of the day.

Blue and French fields on Main Post were named to honor two Fort Benning soldiers who died from injuries incurred while playing polo on those fields, which are used today for youth sports. French Field was dedicated in 1926 in memory of First Lt. Harry W. French, a popular polo player, who died April 14, 1926, after his horse stumbled and rolled over him. Blue Field was dedicated in 1934 to Capt. John W. Blue, who was fatally injured when he was knocked from his pony during a polo game. One of the south's foremost

horsemen, Blue had won various international awards. At the time of his death, he was the only man ever to have won the Clark Machine Gun Trophy twice. Blue also earned many honors in tennis and golf. An interesting note: When officials went to notify Blue's mother of his death, they found her dead.

"It is something of a paradox that the home of the Infantry School should be one of the horsiest posts in the Army," a newspaper editor wrote in 1933. "With the possible exception of (Fort) Riley, the mecca toward which all true believers face when they worship their four-legged god, Benning leads them all in the number and variety of all its mounted activities."

If you were the wife of an officer serving on Fort Benning, you would be expected to take classes in the care and feeding of a horse if you wanted him to succeed at his career. We were not politically correct by today's standards, but we were a lot of fun.

The Campbell King Horseshow Bowl hosted the Fort Benning Easter Sunrise Service in 1948. More than 3,000 people from across the Chattahoochee Valley attended the service, and a thousand soldiers were seated on the field, forming the shape of a cross.

The Campbell King Horseshow Bowl hosted its first show in May 1930. The bowl, which consisted of two rings set in an amphitheater surrounded by shade trees, was named for Brig. Gen. Campbell King, the post commandant who did the most to promote horsemanship and post beautification during his tenure as commandant from 1929-1933.

Located on the northwestern edge of Main Post near the Chattahoochee River, the bowl was primarily used for horse shows and polo matches, but it was also the site of many concerts and Easter Sunrise services, attracting as many as 10,000 people throughout the 30s, 40s and 50s. Gen. George Patton used the arena on many occasions while stationed at Fort Benning.

One of the last great activities at the horse bowl was a concert performed by the Columbus-Phenix City-Fort Benning Bicentennial Band in 1976. After that, the bowl fell into disrepair and was not used again until 2019, when it was renovated to celebrate the centennial anniversary of Fort Benning. It is open now to traffic and once again available for sporting events and picnics.

If I had to identify the greatest or most prolific myth about Fort Benning, it has to be the horseshow bowl. I lost count long ago of the people who have asked me about the slave bowl tucked into the hilly woodlands along the banks of the Chattahoochee River. A popular running trail passes right by the bowl, and the sight of what could be construed as an auction site from

The Campbell King Horseshow Bowl

years gone by occasionally stops them in their tracks. It's easy to understand the mistake but not logical to think anyone was traipsing out to the hinterlands to participate in slave trade, when they could do so conveniently in Columbus, and you will be hard-pressed to find evidence of a "bowl" being used anywhere in the United States for slave auctions.

On Feb. 3, 1943, the USS Dorchester, a troop ship full of American soldiers on their way to Europe, was sank by a German torpedo. Aboard were four Army chaplains who gave their life vests – and their lives – to save civilians and military personnel on the ship. The chaplains, Methodist minister George Fox, Rabbi Alexander Goode, Catholic priest John Washington, and the Reverend Clark Poling of the Reformed Church in America, helped soldiers into life rafts and sacrificed their own life vests when the supply ran out. Survivors reported the "Four Immortal Chaplains" linked arms, said prayers and sang hymns as they went down with the ship. Fort Benning's Field of the Four Chaplains is dedicated to these men. The field is located next to The Infantry Center Chapel on Main Post.

CHAPTER 25

The Wells Plan

In the earliest days of the installation, after the end of the War to End All Wars, soldiers did what soldiers do when they're not training for war. They focused on sports and fitness.

Maj. Gen. Briant Harris Wells

As the commandant of Fort Benning from 1923 to 1926, Maj. Gen. Briant Harris Wells was responsible for the first major period of growth and development. He established the Wells Plan that plotted "districts" across Main Post and emphasized the construction of permanent buildings, landscaping, and sound forest management.

Wells had native trees transplanted alongside the roads on Main Post and pink crepe myrtles and mimosas planted at Riverside and the surrounding neighborhoods. Trees were planted twice as close as normal to achieve a wooded effect quickly, and soldiers attended classes on the general care of trees and tree preservation. Most of the mature trees we enjoy on Main Post today were planted as part of the Wells Plan.

Wells also emphasized the importance of recreation for the troops, directing the construction of several sporting facilities in what he referred to as the athletic district. Today, the Briant Wells Field House, Gowdy Field and Doughboy Stadium are located two blocks from the post's first gymnasium, which has long since been converted to serve another purpose.

Maj. Gen. Wells was quite a character, a West Point graduate, and the veteran of three wars and the Pancho Villa Expedition. He was born in Utah Territory in 1871, the son of the mayor of Salt Lake City. His father was an apostle in Mormon Church, a polygamist with 38 children. Wells' siblings included Heber Wells, first governor of the State of Utah; Elizabeth Wells Cannon, a prominent women's suffragist, and noted Utah politician Rulon S. Wells.

Well's beautification initiative extended beyond the post's physical features. He personally inspected the uniform of every soldier on post.

At the beginning of the 1932 Fort Benning football season, it was announced that the team from the 66th Infantry Regiment would no longer be the Tankers; from now on, they are the "Ironclad Doughboys."

CHAPTER 26

Doughboys

In so many ways the sports district was the hub of activity and entertainment for soldiers and their families in 1925. We were an Army focused on fitness and fun. In the fall of the year, the Doughboys were gearing up for an exciting season that would include matchups against the University of Alabama, Georgia Tech and a number of other colleges and military teams.

The archways under the stadiums housed offices, stores and businesses, like the post's brand-new Beauty Shoppe. An advertisement in the post newspaper encouraged girls to make an appointment with "our expert hair bobber" before the big game. Though the short, blunt controversial Page Boy style was making

The towers on the west end of Doughboy Memorial Stadium were added in 1929 to house offices.

waves across the country, hair bobbing was generally frowned upon in military circles, where social protocols were rigidly conservative. Bob your hair if you dare. A songwriter asked:

Why do you bob your hair, girls? You're doing mighty wrong.

God says it is a glory, and you should wear it long.

You spoil your lovely hair, girls, to keep yourself in style.

Before you bob your hair, girls, just stop and think a while.

Doughboy Stadium was so much more than a commercial enterprise or social center.

The word "Doughboy" was a slang term used for Infantrymen during World War I, much like we use the word "grunt" today. Some say the word was derived from "dough ball," a type of button worn on Infantry overcoats in the early 1800s. Others believe it was first used in the Mexican-American War (1846-48) when U.S. Infantrymen marching through Northern Mexico were covered in clay dust, much like the adobe buildings in the region. The locals referred to them as "adobe boys", which was eventually translated as "doughboys."

However it originated, the word was used fondly by the American population after World War I. When Fort Benning constructed a football stadium in 1925, it was officially dedicated as Doughboy Memorial Stadium, and it was funded by contributions from soldiers around the world who wanted to raise a great monument to the fallen Doughboys of WWI.

Gen. John J. Pershing poured the first concrete in 1924 during the groundbreaking ceremony. The dedication of Doughboy Stadium was celebrated on October 17, 1925, with a game between the Blue Tide of Fort Benning and a team from Oglethorpe University before a crowd of 9,000. Fort Benning's 27-6 victory foreshadowed a lengthy period of success for Fort Benning football.

The story goes that Dwight D. Eisenhower hoped to attend the Naval Academy, and when those hopes were dashed, he went with plan B, West Point, where he poured his energies into football after finding school rules tedious and the classes boring. Eisenhower, who earned five stars before becoming president of the United States, suffered a knee injury so bad, it ended his college football career and threatened his military career when an Army doctor recommended he not receive a commission.

Doughboy Stadium towers under construction in 1929.

Eisenhower was eventually given an Infantry commission in 1915, but he was repeatedly denied requests to see combat in World War I. Instead, he was pressured to coach football. When Maj. Eisenhower arrived at Fort Benning in 1926, he let it be known he wanted nothing to do with the football program. He was promptly made assistant coach to the Fort Benning Doughboys. A marker on Vibbert Avenue tells us Maj. Dwight D. Eisenhower helped lead the Doughboys to an All-Army championship in 1926.

Fort Benning quickly earned a reputation as a contender among colleges throughout the Southeast. The 1946 Doughboys team, coached by Capt. Bill Meeks, outscored opponents 353 to 45 in six games and captured the Service Championship. Meeks went on to work with the Dallas Cowboys.

Doughboy Stadium

Perhaps the greatest of all the Doughboy teams was the 1962 undefeated squad, led by Pat Dye, future coach of Auburn. Two years later, the Washington Touchdown Club named Dye Army Player of the Year.

The success of the Doughboys waned when Fort Benning soldiers were called to fight in Vietnam. The installation fielded post teams until 1983, when the decision was made to disband the team in favor of a strong intramural program, and then resurrected the Doughboy program in 2011 for a few years. Today, those archways house the post's sports, fitness, and aquatics programs.

COMPANY "H"
29TH U.S. INFANTRY
FORT BENNING, GEORGIA

September 3, 1929.

MEMORANDUM TO: The Company Commander.

Request permission to get married.

NORBERT L. CRAINE,
1st Sergeant.

1st Ind.
201-Craine, Norbert L. (Enl)
(9-3-29)
Company H, 29th Infantry, Fort Benning, Ga.,
Sept. 3, 1929, - to: 1st Sgt. Norbert L. Craine.

Permission to get married granted.

O. W. REED,
Captain, 29th Infantry,
Commanding.

In the 1920s, when so many young men came of age on Fort Benning, weekends were spent courting the local ladies, who often traveled in groups to the new post to attend "hops" at the service club. Come payday weekend, Fort Benning soldiers headed into Columbus with a weekend pass and a pocket full of cash to dine and dance and, if they were lucky, find a sweetheart to call their own. By the mid 1920s, Fort Benning had earned the nickname "Mother-in-Law of the Army," because so many soldiers left Fort Benning with a new bride by their side. Back then, a soldier didn't marry without written permission from his commander. Here is a photo of First Sgt. Norbert Craine, H Company, 29th Infantry, and a letter he wrote to his company commander in 1929 requesting permission to marry. It was granted. (#lovewins!)

CHAPTER 27

Hankus-Pankus Gowdy

So many donations came in for the construction of Doughboy Stadium that excess funds were used to build Gowdy Baseball Field.

It was named in honor of Sgt. Harry "Hank" Gowdy, the first major league baseball player to enlist in WWI. He served with the 42nd Rainbow Division and saw action in all the unit's major battles.

His regimental commanding officer, Col. B.W. Hough, said Gowdy was one of his top men. "Every outfit ought to have somebody like Hank," Hough said. "The boys idolize him, and he gets them all stirred up with his baseball stories. He helps 'em forget about the terror of war. He carried the flag and ... he was one of them who heaved gas bombs at the enemy ... he was fantastic!"

Sgt. Harry "Hank" Gowdy

Gowdy went back to the majors after the war and was playing for the New York Giants when Fort Benning celebrated the dedication of Gowdy Field in March 1925. Gowdy threw out the first pitch in an exhibition game between the Giants and the Washington Senators on Gowdy Field. The Giants won.

Gowdy Field

It was vindication, of sorts, for Gowdy, who committed what is considered to be among the greatest errors in baseball history the year before, during game seven of the World Series between the Giants and the Senators. With the score tied at three in the twelfth inning, Washington's Muddy Ruel lifted a high pop-up in foul territory right behind home plate and it looked to be an easy out.

Gowdy, the catcher that day, tracked the ball and tossed his mask aside, anticipating an easy catch. As luck would have it, he stepped on the mask. "It held me like a bear trap," said Gowdy, who fell to the ground and missed the catch. Ruel then hit a double and scored the winning run to give Washington the World Series championship that year.

After a fairly successful career behind home plate, Gowdy became a coach for the Giants, the Braves and the Reds. At the onset of WWII, he did it again; Gowdy left his job for the Army at the age of 53.

On January 23, 1943, newspapers across the country reported that "Hankus-Pankus Hank Gowdy had resigned as coach for the Cincinnati Reds and would return to the Army, this time as a captain, and he would be assigned to Fort Benning to serve with the Special Services Branch where he would manage the post's athletics programs."

Gowdy is believed to be the only big-league baseball player to serve in both wars, but he's not the only big leaguer to serve at Fort Benning. When I was a reporter, I wrote frequently on Fort Benning history and spent a lot of time in the basement of the Infantry Museum, where I got a look at some great treasures that will likely never be found on display in the museum, for lack of space and relevance. Those treasures included a penciled roster from Gowdy Baseball Field with Whitey Ford's name on it.

Whitey Ford is pictured on the right while training on Fort Benning in 1951.

Jackie Robinson and Chuck Stobbs also played on Gowdy Field while serving on Fort Benning.

In 2005, Cal Ripkin Jr. was the guest of honor at the Gowdy Field rededication ceremony. The two-time All-Star MVP for the Baltimore Orioles teamed up with Wisk Laundry Detergent to host the "Win a Dream Field" contest. The Fort Benning community was a grand prize winner, having purchased mass quantities of Wisk, and the prize was a make-over for the field, which had fallen into disrepair in the 80 years since it's construction. Ripkin threw the first pitch – using a ball delivered by a member of the Silverwings Parachute Exhibition team – in a game of fast ball with Fort Benning school children.

Today, Gowdy Field is used for intramural softball and the occasional tournament.

In 1928, the Infantry School News printed a list of interesting grievances received by the War Risk Insurance Bureau during World War I:

• "I haven't heard from my John since he was sent to constipation camp in Germany."

• "I did not receive my husband's pay, so I will have to live an immortal life."

• "My Bill has been put in charge of a spittoon. Will I get more money?"

CHAPTER 28

Benning Booms

The red-brick Dutch Colonial style duplexes on Austin Loop, Sigerfoos, and Wold Avenue were built in 1923-25, making them the oldest homes on Fort Benning today. These were the first permanent houses built for married field grade officers. Like most of the post's early construction, they reflect careful planning with consideration for aesthetics and community. The fronts of the houses on Austin Loop faced the central courtyard, and the backs would today be considered the front, facing the paved road.

A post reporter speculated that the building plans, with those steeply pitched "made-to-shed-snow roofs," were surely intended for a military installation up north, and it must have been a mix-up that resulted in Fort Benning receiving these blueprints. That was not the

The 18 duplex, Dutch Colonial style quarters on Austin Loop were built in 1923-24 for company grade officers. Dwight and Mamie Eisenhower lived at 206 Austin Loop from 1926 to 1927 when he was a major.

case, of course, but I like to point out that those steeply pitched roofs seem to work; you hardly ever see snow on them. Dutch Colonial was the style common to new construction on most Army installations in the south prior to the 1930s.

The Quartermaster in charge of construction was very frustrated with the contractor throughout the process, as was reported in the project summation: "The contractor required constant prodding by the constructing Quartermaster to keep the job moving and even then did not seem able to make the required progress. He did not grasp the magnitude of the job early enough to have any hope of completing on time. He also needed constant reminders about cleaning up after finishing each unit and in this respect was unsatisfactory.

The carpenter work was not of the best. The plasters were good workmen and made a fine piece of work of the exterior stuccoing in particular. The painters were sloppy and needed much watching and constant prodding to keep the job neat and clean. The contractor appeared not to be a specialist on fine residence work, and the work as a whole, while presenting a pleasing appearance, is not of the highest class."

A Dutch Colonial Duplex on Austin Loop

Miller Loop came next. That's the neighborhood tucked behind Army Community Services in Building 7, which was originally the first consolidated school for children on Fort Benning. As part of the Wells' Plan district design, the new school, the post chapel and all family services were located near family housing.

The school was built in 1931 and called The Fort Benning Children's School, because the Army is creative like that. Troops built the school using $29,000 in private funding, mostly contributed by the soldiers, who also paid tuition to ensure the school was staffed.

The McIver Duplexes During Construction

Those 30 giant fourplexes between Lumpkin and First Division are known as White Elephants. Today, it's common to play some version of Dirty Santa at Christmastime, where participants exchange gifts they find useless or tasteless or humorous. That game was borne of a tradition called the white elephant gift exchange. At that point, the term referred to anything that might be classified as an oddity, perhaps something hard to explain or justify, and the concept of very

Before Congress funded permanent housing, soldiers built their own homes, such as the one pictured here in 1923, during the construction of the McIver duplexes you see in the background.

large homes connected in any design other than a brownstone was new and curious in this country, especially in the south, when Fort Benning officials broke ground on the one million dollar project of constructing housing for student officers in 1933. Someone referred to those fourplexes as white elephants, and the name took on a life of its own. Today, you might hear someone refer to any or all of the large white Spanish-style quarters on Main Post as white elephants, but historically, the name was used to describe those fourplexes.

The homes on Rainbow Avenue were completed in the 1930s also, and contrary to popular belief, the road was not named for the colorful houses; it was the other way around. Rainbow Avenue is dedicated to the soldiers of the 42nd Rainbow Division. It was an unusual case of creativity that led the architect to break from tradition and paint the homes anything other than white. Tradition and assimilation are valued as critical to cohesion and good order in the military, and I don't disagree with that, but I do appreciate the man with moxie to paint those houses like a pastel rainbow. How do I know it was a man? Well, as one young Army wife complained in 1935, no one in his right mind would paint a house pink - it clashed terribly with her red hair.

In those early days, when all those grand homes were completed, one of the perks of living on post was the door-to-door commissary service. In front of each house or somewhere on each street stood a wooden box, much like a mailbox, and that's where you would deposit your order for the commissary, a list of the groceries you wished to have delivered to your door. The commissary had a garden, too, and Fort Benning had a cattle ranch, so dining on Fort Benning was originally a farm-to-table experience.

On Halloween night in 1932, a "troupe of juvenile ghosts" played a trick on Fort Benning families, according to the post newspaper, and the results "were almost tragic." Halloween fell on a Monday in 1932, and Tuesday morning "found strange and twisted orders in many of the boxes." The commissary tried to straighten out the situation, but a few families "confessed to being in a positively foodless state."

If the 1920s were marked by struggle for appropriations, the 30s ushered in a period of what could be considered lavish spending on the young Army post, given the state of the nation's economy. In 1933, Fort Benning was allotted $6,352,000 by the Public Works Administration for building projects across the post. By the mid-1930s, Fort Benning was booming with construction.

Two Civilian Conservation Corps camps were located here, which effectively grew the post population with a civilian army of workers skilled in construction. The CCC program, launched in 1933 as part of President Roosevelt's New Deal, brought thousands of young men to Fort Benning, where they were trained and dispatched across the southeast for a variety of construction projects, mostly in state and national parks. The presence of the CCC irked the general post population, since the Army private's base pay was $17.85 a month, and the average CCC worker started at $30.

CHAPTER 29

Pioneers in Petticoats

I have a copy of a letter from a soldier's wife posted in the Camp Benning Infantry School Yearbook in 1921. They called themselves pioneers, those who paved the way for the rest of us, and I think you'll understand why when you read the description of the life of a wife at Camp Benning in 1921. I abbreviated and paraphrased here and there for brevity and because Army language in 1921 was quite another thing. Our unidentified pioneer writes:

When we came to Camp Benning, we did not think it necessary to make elaborate preparations and stock up as if for an exploring expedition. We were wrong. If you are coming next year, bring these few things:

First, at least two children – your own or two orphans. Two children will qualify you for a tent house, four will get you a bungalow.

Pioneers on Horseback

Be sure to bring a shower bath. Some of us have white enameled sinks to bathe the children and one captain uses a garbage can for his bath. We have community bath houses, but it is so discouraging to wait in line (in a bath robe) only to have the hot water fail when your turn comes.

Bring vegetables. Of course we have a commissary which handles good food (except butter), but they will still run on a war-time basis as to prices.

A portable refrigerator is a necessity, because the ice man is temperamental. If he doesn't like the lunch he finds in your refrigerator there will probably be no ice for you.

But servants are plentiful, and for $5 a week you can get a maid who will give you half her time, devoting the other half and all her attention to the soldiers of the labor battalion.

It must be remembered that Camp Benning is still in the growing stage, and that our little difficulties and inconveniences have been such as inevitably befall the pioneers in any new undertaking. The coming school year will find the housing problem solved and complete

permanent utilities installed, and with those two big obstacles removed, we are wondering what people will find to grouch about.

She could not have imagined! If we could resurrect our pioneer and introduce her to social media, I think she'd be surprised and disappointed in what people grouch about. I marvel at her perspective and her good humor. In 1921, the Army had not yet funded housing. These pioneers lived in tents and shacks she so generously referred to as bungalows, and stood in line to use the bath house.

But on the other hand, they hired help for five dollars a week, and you can't beat that. By the time the homes on Austin Loop were completed in 1925, the residents had round-the-clock live-in help. The post newspaper would regularly publish a list of reputable agencies in Columbus where one might find a maid or housekeeper or nanny, whatever you called her, to live at your place Monday through Friday. That's why all the historic homes on post have a space that was originally designated as servant's quarters.

144

And that's why Columbus came to be known early on as the mother-in-law of the Army. Young ladies were eager to work on Camp Benning, where there were thousands of young eligible bachelors decked out in sexy Army uniforms. With WWI barely behind us, Hollywood was capitalizing on the nation's thirst for stories about war heroes, and right here, in their own backyard, local girls found a goldmine. They worked Monday through Friday and, if they were lucky, had a handsome young soldier on their arm come Friday night. And if he got lucky Friday night, you might have to find a new housekeeper Monday morning.

In fact, after The Infantry Center Chapel was built in 1934, it soon became the second most popular wedding venue in the Chattahoochee Valley, second only to the Justice of the Peace. In the 1940s, the chapel was hosting 15 weddings a month, on average.

Back to War

By the early 1940s, we were sending our soldiers to war, again, and here at home, Fort Benning families were doing their part to support the war effort. It was World War II that gave us Rosie the Riveter and thousands just like her. As part of the war conservation efforts, a senior commander's wife encouraged Fort Benning wives to look on the bright side in response to rationing measures that limited the number of shoes they could buy and the types of groceries they could purchase. At this point, they were forced to cut their own bread, a sacrifice common to "wives of the former war," this author noted, referring to Word War I.

If you were an Army wife at Fort Benning at that time, you would have been expected to join the Officers' Wives Club or the Enlisted Wives Club, where you would learn to macramé and make ash trays from clay. You would not have worked outside the house; there was plenty to keep you busy at home, what with ash trays to make and housekeepers to supervise, except maybe to do your part in the Women's Club's Victory Garden Group, which met here for the first time in February of 1943 to plan and plant a community garden.

The women at wartime, at Fort Benning and across the Army, formed their own support networks long before Vietnam, the era that is typically noted for the advent of the contemporary family readiness group. But in the first 50 years of our existence, that network largely centered on our involvement in recreational clubs. It wasn't until the years surrounding the Vietnam War that we began to focus on the need for organized and to some degree, sanctioned, support, beyond the social aspects of our club systems.

SERVICE HUMOR

"S. O. P."

(Standard Operating Procedure)

Who said that "Variety is the Spice of Life?" No doubt 'twas first said by an ARMY WIFE! For the poor girl never knows just where she's at – her home is wherever HE parks HIS hat. She moves every two years into new sets of quarters, during which time she births sons and daughters. She packs up to move to the plains of Nebraska, then Orders are Changed and they go to Alaska. Her house may be a hut with no room for expansion, it may be a tent or perhaps it's a mansion. Then she uncrates the furniture in snow or in rain, and lays the linoleum between labor pains. She wrangles saw horses and builds all the beds, makes curtains of target-cloth she last used for spreads. And during each move – now isn't it strange? The brats invariably catch mumps, measles or mange!

She no more than gets settled when she must dress up pretty, and go to a party and be charming and witty. She must know contract rules, maj jong and chess, and whether a straight or a flush is the best. On every subject she must know how to discourse, she must swim, ski and golf and ride a troop horse. She must know songs and traditions of THE ARMY Corps, and she fast learns all details how HE won the war. She jitterbugs with Lieutenants who always are glamorous – then waltzes with Colonels who are usually amorous. She must drink all concoctions; gin, whiskey and beer – but of course moderately or she'll wreck HIS career.

HE insists on economy, questions every check stub, yet her house must be run like a hotel or club. For she entertains at all hours, both early and late, for any number of guests – eighty or eight. The first of each month there is plenty of cash, so she serves turkey and ham – the last week it's hash. She juggles the budget for a new tropical worsted, though the seams on her own best outfit have bursted. Then she just gets the uniform payments arranged when the blouse is no good. Regulations have changed. One year she has servants and lives like a lady, the next she does her own work and has a new baby. That there'll be a bank balance she has no assurance – it all goes for likker or some damned insurance!

At an age to retire, HE is still hale and hearty, fit as a fiddle, the life of the party; while SHE is old and haggard, cranky and nervous – really a wreck after HIS thirty years' service. But even then, when all's said and done – she STILL believes that Army Life's FUN. She has loved every minute...and why, good grief – she'd have been bored with doctor or merchant chief. But there's one fancy medal – and all Army men wear it...it's their WIVES should have it – that LEGION OF MERIT!

A resilient Army spouse has a sense of purpose and a sense of humor.

In 1964, Fort Benning released a list of summer activities that would offer wives "pleasant diversions and opportunities for self-improvement," including classes in charm and modeling. The curriculum included a study in diction, wardrobe, walking and posture. Just one year later, the wives of 1st Cavalry Division formed the Waiting Wives Club, having recognized a dire need to address communications problems between the Army, the soldier and the family left behind.

In 1964, the Officers' Wives' Club offered classes in charm and modeling.

In that one year, there was a seismic shift in the focus of our networks because there was a seismic shift in our world once again.

You saw the slightly glamorized Hollywood version of this in the movie *We Were Soldiers*, but it's important to note the Waiting Wives Club was one of many predecessors to the family readiness group. There has always been a cohesive culture among Army wives. It is our nature. We have always come together in times of crisis to protect the welfare and morale of our community.

The formalization of the spouses' club did not put an end to all the norms and expectations we might consider quaint today. We recognized that what truly mattered was not our diction or wardrobe, but we didn't forsake the customs and courtesies that gave our community a sense of dignity and grace. You would still receive a letter every year reminding you not to show at the commissary wearing hair rollers. You would still wear gloves to tea.

The 1966 edition of Army Customs for Wives included the following guidelines:

> *The first requirement for an Army wife is adaptability. The service wife must be adept in establishing a homelike atmosphere for her husband and children, then adjust herself to the community as she finds it. As time proceeds, she should do her best to improve conditions and help others, Through the women's clubs, coffee and luncheon groups, PTAs, Youth Activity Clubs and other organizations she may become a helpful citizen and leave her mark for the betterment of the community.*

The following year, the post newspaper's Petticoat Portraits column featured Mrs. Allen Fischer, the chairman of the ceramics shop. "Her creativity is evident in her home," the article said. "Examples of her artwork include a porcelain cigarette set and a fruit bowl." Mrs. Fischer was a licensed beautician taking a break from her career to focus on her husband and two daughters.

Maybe that makes you bristle just a bit? It feels like the language trivializes the role of the military spouse. But these writers were not wrong. This is exactly what we do. We still go where our spouses go. We still put our concerns and careers on the back burner, when need be, to focus on our families and our communities. And we leave our communities in better shape.

CHAPTER 30

A Toast!

Today, the Fort Benning Wives' Club is the Community Spouses Club. We no longer assume all spouses are female. They come to the commissary in hair rollers occasionally and sometimes pajamas. No one's delivering groceries on Fort Benning, sadly, and no one - according to the results of an independent study conducted by me - no one can figure out if macramé is a noun or a verb.

Still, I salute the women who knew Fort Benning when our old homes were new. I love reading about them. I love sharing stories about their way of life. I love that we still hold fast to so many of their meaningful traditions. But I also love today's diverse, independent and resilient take-charge group of tattooed, rock-star military spouses.

In some ways we aren't so different than those early pioneers. We still make great sacrifices. Today our resumes typically include an impressive list of degrees and volunteer experience, but the lack of consistent work history is worrisome and frustrating. No one is telling us how to dress or speak or how to make ashtrays, but we're still keenly aware, whether we like it or not, that we can hinder or enhance our spouses' careers, just as surely as their careers can, and often do, impact ours.

On the other hand, the military population on Fort Benning is also diverse, way beyond the mix of male and female soldiers and beyond Infantry and Armor. Though more than half of the soldiers who enter the Army every year will start right here at Benning at basic training, it is also the Army's premier professional training installation and home to a great variety of courses for officers and noncommissioned officers, nearly 100 in all at the time of this writing, including the most notables - Airborne, Ranger, and Officer Candidate schools. That means many soldiers and their families pass this way again and again in the course of their careers.

If that's your story – if you've lived at Fort Benning long enough to take for granted the impressive array of career-enhancing opportunities here, may I add a basic training graduation ceremony to your bucket list? The experience is good for the soul.

You may wear a scroll on your sleeve or an eagle on your lapel, or you're married to someone who does. Try this. Find a seat in the grandstand on the parade field of the National Infantry Museum on any given Thursday morning, and just watch.

And listen. Listen to the dad who is sitting to your left or the young wife to your right who will cheer with all the conviction of an SEC devotee when his or her soldier walks onto that field.

They probably know nothing – or very little – about what lies ahead. They're not thinking about the badges and patches and certificates he is eyeing. (For the sake of argument, my hypothetical soldier is a he.) All they know or care about is the fact that the greatest soldier in the history of ever is about to walk across the finish line and they get to hug his neck for the first time in a very long time.

Sit and soak that up for a bit, and then reflect on this incredible adventure. From my vantage point, nearly 15 years past Tom's retirement, I can tell you my experience was humbling and challenging, but I wouldn't change it for the world outside that gate. If you don't love your life, email me at bridgettsiteauthor@gmail. com or find me on Facebook or LinkedIn, and let's talk. I'll buy you a cup of coffee, and we'll talk less about history and more about your awesome life, because sometimes you just need to see yourself the way others see you. You come from a long line of pioneers, and that which seems mundane or trivial to you is vital to the fabric of our lives here collectively.

CHAPTER 31

Onward, Soldier!

The year I graduated from Haworth High School in Kokomo, Indiana, the school board stripped my school of its name and identity and handed it over to our number one rival, Kokomo High. The consolidation was designed to save money and resources at a time when midwestern industrial towns were suffering. The steel mill closed, the automotive plants were hanging on by a thread, and Kokomo's population was shrinking. There was no need for two high schools.

I graduated from the last class of Haworth High School. A week later I left town and never moved back. I couldn't tell you a thing about Mr. C.V. Haworth, but when they scrubbed his name from the gymnasium floor, it left me with heartburn that made it less difficult – not easy by any stretch – to cut ties with the only place I had ever called home. Me and 364 of my classmates felt we were robbed of something precious.

Maybe that seems a little dramatic nearly 40 years later, but its where my mind is today, as I struggle to wrap this up. As I'm finishing the final chapter of this book, the conversation at the office and everywhere on social media centers on the renaming of Army installations all across the south, including Fort Benning, which will be Fort Moore by the time you read this.

The 2021 National Defense Authorization Act mandated that all Army installations having Confederate ties to their names must be renamed by the end of 2024. The process is tedious and costly, so most installations are getting an early start.

I will grieve. In fact, I'm already grieving. Fort Benning has been my home, of sorts, for more than two decades. We lived on the installation before Tom retired from active duty, and we've both worked there for 20 years.

Yes, I'm disgusted at the tens of millions of dollars it will take to make these changes, because we're nowhere in the area of fiscal solvency right now. The timing is stupid. But I would be sore if that were not the case. I would be sad if it cost the American taxpayer nothing because I have emotional ties to this place, and emotions are not rational.

I remind you the federal government decided in the early years of the twentieth century to name new military installations located in the south after Confederate generals as a conciliatory gesture aimed at assuaging any lingering bitterness in the decades following the Civil War.

Just as friends of Anna Caroline Benning heckled her lending her support to the new federal installation in 1918, I'm seeing people on social media heckle those who are sore about this change. Surely, if you don't want the name changed, you must support the ideologies of Gen. Benning. You're a racist.

That's silly and untrue.

Change is hard. Hundreds of thousands of veterans, black and white and every shade between, have emotional attachments to Fort Benning. Benning was home during their most formative years; they came of age here. This is where they reached milestones in their careers and developed the strength of character that makes boys into men. Benning prepared them for combat, sent them to war, welcomed them home and gave them a place to heal.

There are others, like me, who enjoyed the cohesive culture of Fort Benning when we were raising our children here. My son once said it was like living in a TV show. (He was thinking more Leave it to Beaver than Married With Children.) We knew Fort Benning at its best. We were the fortunate ones.

A few months back, a coworker asked me what I thought of the plan to rename Fort Benning. He is a black soldier with an eagle on his lapel, so naturally I took a minute to think before speaking. He beat me to it. His career had brought him to Fort Benning several times, and he had been stationed here twice for extended periods. He never knew and never asked where the name Fort Benning originated. The 2021 NDA made him aware of it. He simply didn't care, even now.

The media tells us we should care, and maybe we should.

Those of you who are bruised about this should read up a bit more on the history of Hal and Julia Moore, the great Americans whose name will replace Gen. Benning's. Or watch the movie, *We Were Soldiers*, and you'll learn just enough to appreciate what they did for Army families. (And if you watch closely, you might see some Siters in that movie.)

It's ok to hate that Fort Benning will be "Benning, no Moore." You can hate it and still reject the ideologies that divided our country more than 160 years ago. You can appreciate the selection of the Moores as the new namesakes of this great installation.

Let's move forward together – onward! – shaping the future of an Army installation that shapes the future Army. What is history, really, other than a great collection of object lessons? We learn and grow. The best of our past lies in the service and sacrifice of the soldiers who trained here and the families who lived here. We honor them best when we adopt the same "can do, will do" attitude that saw them through times far more difficult than the angst and inconvenience of rebirth.

Someone asked me the other day if I am comfortable with the title of this book, since it will not be Fort Benning when my book hits the market. This book is full of stories about the first 100 years of this great Army post, when it was called Fort Benning. The funny stories took place on Fort Benning, not Fort Moore. The murders took place on Fort Benning. The ghosts haunted Fort Benning; I guess it remains to be seen if they'll stay for the next chapter.

But I'll stick around for the next chapter, confident that change is somehow healthy if done well, and it's my place to help do it well in my little corner of the world. I hope you'll join me.

Here's to 100 Moore years!

Made in the USA
Monee, IL
28 April 2023

32534298R00085